BUILDING *faith like* THE BROTHER *of* JARED

BRYAN L. BAGGALEY

CFI
An Imprint of Cedar Fort, Inc.
Springville, Utah

ISBN 13: 978-1-4621-3756-5

Published by CFI, an imprint of Cedar Fort, Inc.
2373 W. 700 S., Springville, UT 84663
Distributed by Cedar Fort, Inc., www.cedarfort.com

Library of Congress Control Number: 2020933686

Cover design by Wesley Wheeler

Printed in the United States of America

10 9 8 7 6 5 4 3 2 1

Printed on acid-free paper

This book is dedicated to my grandfather,
James William Linton,
who taught me to love construction,
and to my sister, Jana Joy Baggaley,
who taught me to love the gospel.

Acknowledgments

I am grateful for the help I have received from so many people in writing this book. In 2015, I told my brother Todd Baggaley how the story of the brother of Jared had been an influence in my life. He encouraged me to write it down as testimony for my posterity. That journal eventually became the basis for this book. I am grateful for Todd's inspiration and encouragement.

I must also thank all of those who read through my early manuscripts and offered help, suggestions, and encouragement. Specifically my mother, Ellen Linton Baggaley, and my niece, Anne Trout, who helped me organize and modify my technical writing style into a more interesting and readable format. My neighbor, Neill Marriott, also read through early versions and gave me guidance and recommendations. I have received input and suggestions from many others, including my eleven siblings, their spouses, ward members, and friends.

My eight children have been patient through many versions and manuscripts. They have endured many family home evenings that defaulted into lectures on the subject of the brother of Jared. To avoid my lengthy commentary, my children made sure our family scripture study addressed the Ether chapters when I was away on business. I am grateful for their patience.

Last, I am grateful for my wife, MaryAlice. She is my love and support in all of my endeavors but has especially encouraged me while I have written this book. She has been my chief editor in each manuscript and has helped me find the determination and time to write. The scriptures do not mention the sister-in-law of Jared, but I am convinced that without her, the Jaredites would still be stuck on the seashore.

Contents

And let us make us a name.
—Genesis 11:4

The people of Babel built the world's tallest tower for two purposes:

1. To enter heaven and find a hidden God.
2. To make a name for themselves, known throughout the world.

The brother of Jared left Babel and journeyed to the top of a distant mountain, where, by his faith, heaven's veil was opened and he beheld the living God. Of all the people in the great city of Babel, only one entered heaven and found God. Why was his name hidden from the world?

Introduction

The people of Babel were the most technologically advanced in their time. They were designers and builders, and their economy was based on construction. They designed a tower to reach the heavens and built a city surrounding the tower.

Having lived in Babel, the Jaredites were also designers and builders. They designed vessels to carry live fish and built barges to go beneath the waves of the sea. The intelligence and ingenuity of these people gave them the capacity to design and build "anything which they imagined to do" (Genesis 11:6).

Jesus Christ is the ultimate designer and builder. Raised as a carpenter's son, He knew the construction trades. In His mortal ministry He critiqued the construction of towers and temples and applied these lessons for our learning. In the premortal realm, He built the earth as a classroom for our mortal experience and designed the great plan for our salvation.

My career and my passion are to design and build. I have been a licensed contractor for more than twenty-five years. I have studied design and have both a bachelor's and master's degree in civil engineering. I am a licensed structural engineer. I have engineered several buildings on the BYU campus and designed the structure for the Nauvoo Temple. In 2009 when I read the Lord's direction to the brother of Jared to "go to work and build" (Ether 2:16), I felt inspired to build a new home for my family. I have since worked with my wife and teenagers to design and build our own home—three times. As I have built these homes and designed these buildings, I have pondered about the Jaredites and the barges they constructed as well as the people of Babel and the tower they designed.

My background and experience in design and construction led me into a career of forensic engineering where I now specialize in investigating construction defects and engineering errors. Where previously in my career I had designed and constructed buildings to stand up, I now investigate why they fail or fall down.

My career in investigation increased my fascination with the story of the brother of Jared. In Ether 2:19, the brother of Jared complains that the barges they have built have no light and no air. In my investigations I often evaluate claims of construction defects regarding inadequate ventilation or insufficient light much like the complaints the brother of Jared made regarding the barges. A forensic investigator would seek to determine why these barges were built without adequate light and air, and who was responsible for this oversight. Thus, I began to research and investigate the barges, the builders, and the designer to form a theory that would provide answers to these questions.

Although the barges were perplexing, the real mystery was in the brother of Jared himself. Who was he? What was his background? Why was his name not recorded? Why would such a faithful man falter in his prayers? How was this man able to repent from his lack of prayer and increase his faith such that he could enter into the presence of God? Perhaps the theory I developed regarding the barges would provide answers to these mysteries as well. As I investigated, I came to conclusions that sometimes differed from, or added to, available scholarly explanations. The answers I found were fascinating.

The ideas presented in this book are based on my analytical investigations that present probable answers to the questions and mysteries within the story of the brother of Jared. Given the age of the events and the limited information available, it is impossible to prove any of the ideas presented short of prophetic clarification. As such the conclusions presented are just theories, and any errors in this book are mine.

As members of The Church of Jesus Christ of Latter-day Saints, each of us is entitled to receive inspiration and revelation according to our personal needs. The Spirit of the Lord may inspire one individual with thoughts and inspiration from a scripture and may yet inspire a different individual with a different interpretation or insight. Both interpretations may be appropriate and serve the purposes of the Lord as intended for each specific person. As such, the thoughts and interpretations in this book are my thoughts and interpretations and are not presented as Church doctrine nor as "correct" inspiration. This book is therefore my testimony of how the Lord has used the story of the Jaredites to inspire and bless my family as we have struggled on our journey to seek the promised land.

Chapter 1

THE SEARCH FOR GOD

Many of the world's religions have four common tenants or beliefs that are intended to explain God's existence and the purpose of life. These four common beliefs include the following:

1. There is a God who is all knowing and all powerful.
2. There is a place or existence where God dwells, commonly referred to as heaven.
3. The purpose of this life is to serve as a test to determine if our souls are worthy of attaining heaven after this life.
4. This test must allow us freedom of choice so that our true nature may be revealed. Because of this, it is necessary for Deity to be concealed. Otherwise, the knowledge of God may influence our choices inconsistent with our true nature, invalidating the test.

Since the beginning of time, the determination to discover, uncover, or disprove the existence of God has been the great quest of the ages. Every intellectual inquiry and scientific investigation have been implemented and devoted to the quest to discover God. However, as God has used His matchless power to conceal Himself, no earthly investigation has been capable of proving or disproving the existence of Deity. Some have come to the conclusion that since so many scientific methods have failed to prove the existence of God, God must not exist. Some have gone so far as to teach and even militantly preach the non-existence of God with the audacious assumption that their capacity and ability to discover God is greater than the ability and power of Deity to conceal Himself. Many more come to the conclusion that it is impossible for man to discover God or know God in any capacity. Many of these people have given up on the quest to discover God and have resigned themselves to an agnostic view of life.

People of religious persuasion have learned that just because mankind has no scientific capacity or earthly ability to discover God, does not mean that God does not exist or cannot be known. If God is all powerful, it is certainly possible that God may choose to reveal His reality to those who demonstrate that their nature is compatible with heaven. The revealing of His reality may come in the form of feelings, answered prayers, or miracles that do not compromise freedom of choice but still increase our comprehension of Him. Thus, God may choose to reveal His existence to an individual in a manner comparable with the faith they have demonstrated. Those who develop great faith may even align their nature with Deity such that they could see God and stand in His presence. These individuals, or prophets, under the guidance of God, could then organize a religion to give direction to those who desire to follow. Therefore, a true religion must include a record of prophets who have, in fact, stood in the presence of God, as well as a record of their teachings and direction.

The Old Testament, which is accepted and revered by many world religions, contains the record of Abraham, Moses, and several others who stood in God's presence and have proceeded to lead and teach those who would follow. The New Testament is a record of God Himself walking on earth. Yet, of the thousands of people who interacted with Him, few could see and comprehend His divinity.

The Book of Mormon provides additional examples of prophets who have stood in the presence of God, culminating with the appearance of the Savior to thousands of people. These people witnessed that they had seen and stood in the presence of the Lord.

Since the First Vision of the Prophet Joseph Smith, and throughout the restoration of The Church of Jesus Christ of Latter-day Saints, there have been multiple records of those who have entered into the presence of God. Of all of the teachings of the Restoration, one of the most beautiful is that it is actually God's work, desire, and glory to bring each of His children back into His presence.

The story of the brother of Jared stands out among the records of man's pursuit to discover God and enter His presence. This record contains one of the most detailed encounters of mankind with God when the brother of Jared saw the premortal Jesus Christ. In this encounter, God revealed all things to the brother of Jared, including the past, present, and future.

What makes the story of the brother of Jared even more remarkable is that a short time previously, the Lord chastised the brother of Jared because he ceased to pray for an extended period of time—possibly for a number of years. In the church today some may have labeled the brother of Jared as "inactive" or "fallen away." Yet despite his years of faithlessness, the brother of Jared was able to repent and increase his faith over a short period of time such that he was able to enter into the presence of God and view the visions of eternity.

What brought about this incredible transformation that changed an "inactive" man into one of the greatest prophets of the Book of Mormon? How was a man who hadn't prayed in years able to find the faith necessary to stand in the Lord's presence? What can we learn from his experience that can help us increase our faith so that we can dwell in the presence of God? How can we learn to build our faith like the brother of Jared?

Chapter 2

MORONI AND THE JAREDITE RECORD

At the conclusion of the Book of Mormon, the Nephite people gathered at the Hill Cumorah for one great and final battle with their enemies, the Lamanites. Here, Moroni witnessed the final destruction of all his people, including his father, Mormon, who had been their commander and spiritual leader. Prior to their destruction, Mormon abridged one thousand years of Nephite history into one book written on gold plates, which we now know as the Book of Mormon. With the death of Mormon, the responsibility fell upon Moroni to complete the record and document the final fall of the Nephites:

> Behold, I Moroni, do finish the record of my father, Mormon. Behold, I have but few things to write, which things I have been commanded by my father . . . and I even remain alone to write the sad tale of the destruction of my people. . . .
>
> Therefore I will write and hide up the records in the earth; and wither I go it mattereth not. Behold, my father hath made this record, and he has written the intent thereof. And behold, I would write it also if I had room upon the plates, but I have not; and ore I have none, for I am alone. My father hath been slain in battle, and all my kinsfolk, and I have not friends nor whither to go; and how long the Lord will suffer that I may live I know not. (Mormon 8:1–5)

One of the things that Moroni was commanded to write was an abridgement of a record of the Jaredite people who had inhabited the land prior to the Nephites. Like the Nephites, the Jaredites had migrated from the old world, settled the land of the Americas, and eventually suffered a similar fate as the Nephites due to wickedness and wars. The responsibility for abridging the record of the Jaredites fell upon Moroni:

> And now, I Moroni, proceed to give an account of those ancient inhabitants who were destroyed by the hand of the Lord upon the face of this north country. And I take mine account from the twenty and four plates which were found by the people of Limhi, which is called the Book of Ether. . . . But behold, I give not the full account, but a part of the account I give, from the tower down until they were destroyed. (Ether 1:1–5)

This record contained the history of Jared and his people who left the great tower and city of Babel to gather in a valley northward. In that valley, the Lord came to the people concealed in a cloud and led them through a vast wilderness to a distant seashore, where barges were constructed at the direction of the Lord. These barges would take the Jaredites from the seashore of the old world to the land of the Americas where they would start a new civilization greater than any that existed. The Jaredites would dwell in the Americas for thousands of years, and the people would prosper, become prideful, fight, dwindle, repent, and prosper again. This cycle continued until the end of the record when the people had all become wicked except for one man, the prophet Ether, who compiled the history of his people and recorded the final battles that brought about the Jaredites' demise. Moroni abridged this record of the Jaredites into the book of Ether as contained in the Book of Mormon.

Unlike his father, Mormon, Moroni had little experience in abridging the record of a people. Furthermore, he had no resources to create new plates and little space on the remaining plates to abridge the history of the Jaredites. Due to the lack of space on the plates, many events and details contained in the original record of Ether could not be recorded in Moroni's abridgement.

Writing on the plates was difficult and was accomplished by scratching characters and symbols into the surface of the soft metals (Jacob 4:1). Once the characters were written, there was no opportunity to revise or amend the record. The difficulty of writing in this manner is intimidating. In an age of computers, it is hard for us to comprehend the task placed on Moroni to write the story of these people without opportunity to revise or edit.

Some of the difficulty in writing and abridging is apparent in the early chapters of Moroni's abridgement as he interjects spiritual commentary and prophesies between bursts of record and history. Some of Moroni's commentary includes his concerns that the Gentiles who would receive the record would mock it because of his weakness in writing and the placing of his words. Yet the Lord permitted the record to be written in his language and in his words with the assurance that the meek and the humble would not take advantage of his weakness (see Ether 12:23–25).

Whether by weakness in writing, insufficient space, or by spiritual intent, the initial chapters of the abridgement of Moroni contain many missing details or hints of events that were not fully recorded. The most prominent detail that is missing from the record is the name of the Jaredites' spiritual leader who is only known throughout the record as "the brother of Jared." This nameless man is the prominent figure in the first six chapters of the book. As their spiritual leader, he supplicates the Lord to lead them through the wilderness, directs the building of the barges on the seashore, and leads the people across the ocean to the promised land. Yet in six chapters of scripture his name is not mentioned. Why did Moroni fail to include this important name in the record?

In addition to the missing name of the brother of Jared, the Jaredite journey is full of mysteries and questions that seem to be unanswered. Finding potential answers to these questions could give us greater insight into the purposes of God and His plan for us as His children. In reading the story of the brother of Jared, missing details, mysteries, and questions are left unanswered, such as the following:

1. What is the name of the brother of Jared?
2. Why is the name of the brother of Jared not in the scriptures?
3. What influence did the city and Tower of Babel have on the people and story of the Jaredites?
4. Why is there virtually no record of what happened to the Jaredites during their initial four years on the seashore?
5. Why did the brother of Jared cease praying to the Lord during the four-year time period on the seashore?
6. After four years on the seashore, the Lord instructs Jared to build "barges after the manner which ye have hitherto built" (Ether 2:16). Where and when had the people of Jared built barges previously?
7. Why did the Lord command the people of Jared to build barges that were of such unusual shape and function?
8. If God is perfect, why didn't God's plan for building the barges consider such basic needs as adequate light, air, or a method to steer? How could a perfect God come up with an imperfect plan that did not provide the basic necessities to sustain life?
9. When did the brother of Jared and the people first realize that the barges they were commanded to build had major flaws? Were the people so foolish that they did not notice these flaws until all eight barges were built?[1]
10. Why did the brother of Jared wait until all eight of the barges were complete before asking for the Lord's help to address the flaws?
11. What is the significance of the flaws in the barges and the significance of the way in which the Lord, the brother of Jared, and the people of Jared addressed or reacted to each of these flaws?
12. In what ways are the flaws in the barges pertinent to us today?
13. How did the brother of Jared progress from a state where he had not prayed for an extended time to a state where he had such exceeding faith that he was capable of entering into the presence of God?

14. How were the people of Jared able to progress from being similarly inactive in their faith and content on the seashore to receiving their inheritance within the promised land?

Whether these details and information were left out due to lack of space, difficulty in writing, or spiritual intent is unclear. Finding answers to these questions could provide additional insight into the minds of the people and the intent of the Lord. One method to find possible answers is to use investigative and analytical techniques to evaluate possible solutions or explanations to these questions. These probable solutions may then provide additional spiritual insight into the lives of these people and the workings of the Lord.

Some specific investigative methods may include character and background analysis to evaluate how certain people would have reacted in known situations. We can also compare known outcomes against unknown possible events to determine which events most likely resulted in the known outcome. Another technique is to list all possible answers to a question and use a process of analysis to eliminate proposed solutions that are infeasible or unrealistic. As the great detective Sherlock Holmes pointed out, "once you eliminate the impossible, whatever remains, no matter how improbable, must be the truth."[2]

Of all the questions listed above, the most important for us is to know how the brother of Jared increased his faith to such a degree that he could stand in the presence of God. This is the mystery and goal of every member of the Church—to progress from our present imperfect state to a state where we are redeemed and are worthy to dwell in God's presence. Likewise, it is our goal to help our families build their faith and enable them to receive their inheritance in the celestial kingdom, just as the brother of Jared was able to lead his family into the promised land.

NOTES

1. Throughout this book I often refer to the lack of light and air in the barges as "defects" or "flaws" in the plans for the construction of

the barges. I do this with the understanding that to consider these things "defects" is a worldly view. To man's point of view, a barge built without air or light is certainly a defective or flawed vessel. Yet we know that God is perfect and that all of His plans are perfect—including His plan for the barges. Thus, one purpose of this book is to present an explanation of how a barge that is clearly "defective" to mans limited comprehension is still perfect in God's eternal plan.

2. *The Sign of Four*, Sir Arthur Conan Doyle. This book was the second Sherlock Holmes book originally published by *Lippincott's* monthly magazine in 1890 (United Kingdom). It has been republished several times since then. It is now in the public domain and is available from multiple free sources.

Chapter 3

A CITY AND A TOWER, A SEER AND A TEMPLE

The people of Babel sought to build a city and a tower that would reach the heavens—taller than any tower that had ever been built. Satan himself had put it into their hearts that by building the tower they could attain heaven: "And they said, Go to, let us build us a city and a tower, whose top may reach unto heaven; and let us make us a name, lest we be scattered abroad upon the face of the whole earth" (Genesis 11:4).

Any endeavor to reach heaven is more than just attaining a place. It is an attempt to find a Being. By definition heaven is the place where God dwells. As such, the people of Babel were seeking more than heaven; they were determined to find God.

The people of Babel did not seek to build for the glory of God, but rather with the purpose to uncover God, to expose Him in His hiding place, and establish a back door into the heavenly realm. Furthermore, by building the tallest tower and reaching the heavens they were convinced they would "make a name" for themselves (Genesis 11:4). They were sure that the fame of the tower would spread and the name of their city would be renowned throughout the world. Their leaders sought to be known as the people who discovered God, or disproved His existence. As such, the height of their intended tower was only exceeded by the loftiness of their leaders' pride. Their desire to uncover God and spread their fame was such that they named their city Babel, which means "Babilim" or "gate of God" in the Akkadian tongue.[1]

We commonly read the story of the brother of Jared as it is told in the Book of Mormon, but we forget that the background of the story of the Jaredites begins in Babel as recorded in the book of Genesis. The backstory of the brother of Jared at the Tower of Babel is compelling because every action of pride and wickedness displayed by the people of Babel has a contrasting element of humility and faith ingrained within the record of the Jaredites.

The people of Jared abandoned the land of Babel and sought to obtain their own land, the land of promise. In their quest, they followed the Lord on a journey that led them to a distant seashore. At the seashore another building project commenced under the direction of the Lord. Unlike Babel, this project would not include the building of a tower with the intent to ascend higher than any human had ever gone. In contrast, this project would entail the construction of barges or vessels that would take the people of Jared into the midst of the sea, below the depths where any man had ever descended. Unlike the exalted pride of the leaders of Babel, this voyage could not be undertaken unless the people of Jared exercised faith and humbled themselves below the depths of the deepest ocean.

Man conceived the construction of the tower with the purpose of discovering God in His hiding place. God conceived the construction of the barges to build faith in the brother of Jared and prepare him to enter His presence. The culmination of man's project to build the barges and God's project to build the man came when the brother of Jared brought stones of clear glass before God and witnessed the finger of the Lord as He extended His hand to touch the stones. The touch of the Lord's finger gave light to the refined stones. The vision of the Lord's finger brought redemption to the refined man. Through this experience, the brother of Jared had indeed entered into the heavens and into the presence of God Himself, the Lord Jesus Christ.

The people of Babel audaciously sought to build a tower in order to discover God and bring fame to their name. However, the people of Babel only accomplished part of their goal as the city of Babel today is indeed known throughout the world for their failure to build a tower and discover God. As such, the word *Babel* has become synonymous with the Hebrew word *balal*, meaning "confusion" or "incomprehension."

The brother of Jared achieved the impossible goal of the people of Babel. He found the gate of God, the path to heaven, and entered into the presence of the Lord. The brother of Jared accomplished exactly what the people of Babel intended to do. Yet rather than use this incredible accomplishment to make a name for himself, the actual name of the brother of Jared remains unmentioned and unknown throughout the record.

The humble faith of a nameless man accomplished more than all the efforts of the glory-seeking inhabitants of the great city of Babel. The failure of Babel and its tower teaches us that we cannot find God or enter into His presence by taking pride in the reputation of our own works or our own name. From the height of the tallest mountain of which man can ascend to the depth of the deepest ocean into which man may descend, there is only one name by which man can enter into the presence of God, the name of the Lord Jesus Christ.

> Wherefore how great the importance to make these things known unto the inhabitants of the earth, that they may know that there is no flesh that can dwell in the presence of God, save it be through the merits, mercy and grace of the Holy Messiah. (2 Nephi 2:8)

NOTE

1. Genesis 10:8–10 informs us that Babel was originally built by the mighty hunter Nimrod, who also established three other cities, including Erech, Calneh, and Accad. The Akkadian language was named for the city of Accad (also spelled Akkad) and was spoken throughout the Akkadian Empire in the Mesopotamian area. As such it would appear that Accad was the city that succeeded to make a name for itself that was known throughout the region.

Chapter 4

THE NAME OF THE BROTHER OF JARED

On July 26, 1834, a son was born to Elder Reynolds Cahoon in Kirtland, Ohio. Sometime thereafter, Brother Cahoon saw the prophet Joseph Smith passing his door. Brother Cahoon called to Joseph and requested that he give his son a name and a blessing. Joseph agreed to do so and proceeded to bless the child and give him the name of Mahonri Moriancumer. When Joseph Smith finished the blessing, he turned to Elder Cahoon and informed him the name given to his son was the name of the brother of Jared. Joseph then said the Lord had revealed the name to him during the child's blessing.[1]

In 1834, the Church was still very new and had recently moved to Kirtland, Ohio. In Kirtland, Joseph Smith was regularly receiving revelation that would guide the new church. Joseph's revelations were compiled into a new book of commandments that would be fully printed in 1835 as the Doctrine and Covenants. The contents of the book included several revelations giving clarifications to the doctrine of the Bible. Furthermore, the second edition of the Book of Mormon would be published a short time later in 1837. The second edition would include many minor grammatical corrections and corrections of typesetting errors. If the missing name of the brother of Jared had been caused by human error or oversight, Joseph Smith could have made a minor correction to the Book of Mormon to include the name or added a footnote to the record. Alternatively, Joseph Smith could have published this revelation in the new edition of the Doctrine and Covenants. Yet these "corrections" were not made. As such, the revelation of the name of the brother of Jared remains rather obscure in the records of Church history.[2]

Several scholars have opined on the reason the name of the brother of Jared was not included in the Book of Mormon.[3] Some have speculated that possibly the name Mahonri Moriancumer could not be written in the reformed Egyptian language used by Moroni. Others have preferred the notion that since Ether was the original author of the Jaredite record and was a direct descendant of Jared rather than Mahonri Moriancumer, Ether's record was intended to be only a record of Ether's direct family line.

If either of these were the case it would seem a minor correction or footnote to the Book of Mormon to include the name of Mahonri Moriancumer would have added knowledge to the record. Yet no modification was made. As such, we can conclude that the name was not withheld from the Book of Mormon by human error, family prejudice, or difficulty of writing. It would seem the name was withheld by spiritual intent as reflected by Joseph Smith's original direct translation.

Many scholars have also noted that the Apostle John withheld his own name in his record of the Gospel of John out of modesty and that the brother of Jared may have intended the same. The brother of Jared certainly saw and experienced the grandiose pride of the leaders of Babel as they boasted that they would build their tower and exalt their own name. Given his background in Babel, it seems likely that it was by his own choice that his name was not recorded. Out of respect for this choice, the remainder of this book will refer to him as "the brother of Jared" rather than by his name "Mahonri Moriancumer," except where his actual name becomes specific to the discussion. By this choice, the brother of Jared may have intended to demonstrate that in order to attain the presence of God we must place our own will and our own name on the altar of sacrifice before we take upon us the name of the Lord Jesus Christ.[4]

NOTES

1. "The Jaredites," *The Juvenile Instructor,* May 1, 1892, 282.
2. Any commentary on the brother of Jared must include the story of Joseph Smith receiving revelation that the name of the brother of Jared was Mahonri Moriancumer. However, it appears that the brother of Jared intentionally decided not to include his own name in the record for his own spiritual reasons. Out of respect for his decision, the remainder of this book will continue to refer to him as "the brother of Jared" rather than Mahonri Moriancumer, except where his name is pertinent to the discussion.
3. Daniel H. Ludlow noted several possible reasons the brother of Jared's name was not recorded in the book. See *A Companion to Your Study of the Book of Mormon* (Salt Lake City: Deseret Book, 1972), 310.
4. Cecil O. Samuelson suggested that the record is "more fundamentally about Jesus Christ" than about the brother of Jared or the Jaredites. Therefore, there were likely spiritual reasons for withholding his name from the record. See *Heroes of the Book of Mormon* (Salt Lake City: Bookcraft, 1995), 185.

Chapter 5

BEGINNING AT BABEL

In the fall of 1996, I stood with my new wife on the site where the Nauvoo Temple had previously been built but had subsequently been destroyed by the work of devious men and Mother Nature. While standing there discussing the former temple with a site missionary, he turned to us and prophesied that the temple would be rebuilt and that President Hinckley would be the one to do it. In general conference of April 1999, President Hinckley stunned the members when he announced the Church would reconstruct this beautiful temple.

As a young engineer, I was working for the firm selected to do the structural engineering on the Nauvoo Temple. Subsequently, I was assigned to the team responsible for designing the concrete and steel that would become the supporting structure of the building. For several months the preliminary plans for the Nauvoo Temple sat on my desk as I developed the computer model to ensure the concrete walls and steel tower could support the weight of the floors, as well as resist earthquake and wind forces. Like Oliver Cowdery when he was scribe for the Book of Mormon, I often thought to myself that these were days "never to be forgotten" (JS—H 1:71; see footnote). The design and construction of the Nauvoo Temple would become a highlight of my career. The height of the temple from the ground to the top of the angel Moroni would reach 162 feet. This would be the tallest structure I would ever design.

My experience as a design structural engineer made me appreciate the technology and expertise required to build skyscrapers and great cities. The feat of constructing the world's tallest building is a task of monumental proportions. To build such a building requires an extraordinary amount of designing, engineering, planning, financing, construction leadership, and material and labor management. As in Babel's time, the people and the cities who accomplish such feats today become world famous and the buildings become iconic in their symbolism and display of wealth and knowledge. Such iconic buildings include the Egyptian pyramids, Eiffel Tower, Empire State Building, Twin Towers, Sears or Willis Tower, Petronas Towers, Taipei 101, and the Burj Khalifa. These buildings have brought fame and notoriety to their designers and cities.

The competition to build ever higher and notorious buildings continues today as it has since the dawn of time. The first record of a people who attempted to build the world's tallest building occurred in the city of Babel where it was recorded that the people were determined to build a city and tower that would reach into the heavens (see Genesis 11:3–9). The record even includes an account of the materials that were to be used and identified them as fired brick and bitumen tar referred to in the Bible as "slime." The use of these advanced materials in their day demonstrated the acuity the people had attained in engineering and construction as well as designing, planning, and managing materials and labor. The determination of the people of Babel to achieve this goal and exalt their name exceeded all other people up to that time in the history of the world. Even the Lord acknowledged the capacity of the people to design and build this tower when He stated, "The people are one . . . and nothing will be restrained from them which they have imagined to do" (Genesis 11:6).

The Bible teaches us that the Lord confounded the languages and scattered the people to stop the construction of the tower. However, the Book of Mormon gives us additional insight into the minds of the people and the intent of the Lord. Specifically, Helaman 6:28 teaches us that it was Satan who put it into the hearts of the people to build the tower in order to get to heaven. What purpose could Satan have had with the tower? Surely Satan knew that the people of Babel could not build a tower that could enter heaven or expose the true and living God. It is possible that Satan intended to use the tower to deceive the people into believing they had proven there was no heaven and no God. It may have been that Satan intended for the wicked leaders of Babel to assume the title of Deity and proclaim they were gods. Perhaps Satan even planned to present himself at the top of the tower as the god of this world. The Lord's wrath with Satan and his followers caused Him to confound the languages and scatter the people (see Ether 1:33). By confounding the languages and scattering the people, the Lord protected His children from Satan's intended tower of deception.

Babel was an advanced civilization for its time. The technology, ingenuity, and education of the people of Babel were comparable to people who would come thousands of years later. Construction with fired brick, as used to build the ancient tower, is still prominent today. Animals and wagons would have been necessary to transport construction materials as well as commodities to sustain the city and construction. Boats on the Euphrates or Tigris rivers would have facilitated trade between civilizations. These methods of construction, transportation, and commerce used in Babel would be the standard for thousands of years. Even the early Latter-Day Saint pioneers built buildings with fired brick and traveled by wagons and oxen that were essentially the same as the construction methods and modes of transportation used at the time of Babel.

We can also learn much about the people of Jared from the planning and preparations they made for their journey as documented in Ether 2:13. The recorded list of provisions included flocks, seeds, and bees, which would provide meat, grain, and honey for the people during their journey to the promised land. It is clear that these people meticulously planned their journey and desired to prepare in every way possible. The supplies that the Jaredites were able to gather for the journey indicates they were people of means and resources. As such the Jaredites likely came from the middle or upper classes of the people of Babel.

These verses similarly teach us that the Jaredites were people of skill and ingenuity. The record indicates they had hunting and fishing skills that would be needed on their journey. It is noted that they built and laid snares for the fowls of the air and even built a vessel in "which they did carry with them the fish of the waters" (Ether 2:2).

Designing and constructing a water-tight vessel capable of carrying fish over dry land is certainly no small feat given the limitations of their day. Anyone who has carried a bucket of water will realize how difficult it is to move the bucket without the water sloshing over the sides. Building a vessel to carry live fish on an overland journey would have required they contain the water as it moved and create a mini mobile ecosystem capable of providing oxygen, food, and light to sustain the life of the fish. There is no record of other journeys—including Moses and his people, the Nephites, or even more modern pioneers—where the organization and planning included transporting live fish. It would seem that Moroni himself was impressed with their ingenuity, creativity, and construction ability such that he would include these observations in his limited writings.

In Ether 1:3–4 and Ether 8:9 we learn that the Jaredites brought with them a written record of the history of the world from Adam down to the time of the tower. This written record was also updated and maintained during the Jaredites' crossing of the sea and during their time in the new land. In ancient times such records were only kept, owned, and maintained by highly educated people or leaders of a synagogue. The fact that the brother of Jared had access to these records and had the education to read and write them is an indication he was possibly a leader or a priest in a synagogue. Ether 1:41 also states that the brother of Jared owned flocks, which a priest would have needed to offer sacrifice in behalf of the people according to the ancient commandments. Jared and his people routinely asked the brother of Jared to pray in their behalf. This may seem unusual today as we are instructed to pray ourselves. However, in ancient times, the priest would routinely offer animal sacrifice, or incense prayers, in behalf of the people of his congregation similar to the sacrifice and offerings in the law of Moses offered by the Levites in behalf of all Israel.

Given this background and record, we know that the Jaredites were a highly intelligent people from the middle or upper classes of the people of Babel. They were planners and problem solvers who could foresee and predict the calamities coming upon the people of Babel. They planned for an extended journey over land and sea unlike any journey that had ever before been undertaken up to that date. Furthermore, these people had been immersed in the foremost construction-oriented society of their day and could invent and build unusual vessels as had never before been constructed.

When the Lord looked on the people of Babel, He noted that "nothing could be restrained from them which they have imagined to do" (Genesis 11:6). Yet of all the people in Babel, only a select few were chosen by the Lord to make the difficult journey to the promised land. These chosen Jaredites were among the ones who had the capacity to accomplish anything they imagined.

Unlike the wicked leaders of Babel who used their abilities and talents to build a deceptive tower, the Jaredites sought to use their talents to obtain the Lord's promised land. Thus, the wickedness of Babel is contrasted by the righteousness of the Jaredites. The Lord uses this contrast to demonstrate the blessings of righteousness compared to the consequences of evil. Every wicked plan or desire in the story of Babel has a contrasting blessing of righteousness found in the story of the Jaredites. The following table identifies a list of the Lord's blessings for the righteous people of Jared in contrast to the downfall of Satan's wicked kingdom of Babel. Many of these identified contrasts will become the basis for discussion or chapters in this book as we investigate and expand the practical and spiritual implications of these lessons.

Babel	Jaredites
The people of Babel sought to enter heaven.	The Jaredites entered into the promised land.
The leaders of Babel sought to enter God's presence.	The brother of Jared saw God and entered His presence.
The people of Babel sought to build a tower that would extend higher into the heavens than any building ever built.	The Jaredites built barges that would descend deeper into the sea than any vessel ever built.
The leaders of Babel sought to make their name famous.	The brother of Jared's name was not made known in the record.
The capacity of the people of Babel was such that they could do anything they imagined.	God's plan for His people was more incredible than the Jaredites' greatest imagination.
With one decree from God, the construction of the Tower of Babel was thwarted and the people of Babel were scattered.	By one touch from God's finger the barges were redeemed from their lack of light and the Jaredites were united.
The language of the people of Babel was confounded to stop their attempt to discover God and His secrets.	The brother of Jared discovered all the secrets of God but recorded it in a confounded language.
The failures of Babel to build their tower, attain heaven, and discover God are known throughout the world.	The vision of the brother of Jared was written in the sealed portion of the golden plates and remains unknown to the world.
Never had there been greater pride than was found in the leaders of Babel.	Never had there been greater humility and faith than was found in the brother of Jared.

The leaders of Babel thought that their ability to discover God was greater than God's ability to conceal Himself.	The brother of Jared's faith was so great that God could not keep Him from beholding within the veil.
The Tower of Babel was designed by men to reach heaven but was void of spiritual light.	The barges were designed by God for man to reach the promised land. They were filled with light that was given by His touch.
The city of Babel thought itself to be the "gate of God."	Baptism is the true gate to the heavenly path. The Jaredites' barges were immersed in the sea on their journey to the promised land symbolic of baptism.
Satan put these things into their heart.	God led and directed His people continually.
The people of Babel were scattered and the city left desolate due to the hand of Satan.	The Jaredites were redeemed and saved in the promised land by the hand of Jesus Christ.

Chapter 6

THE GEOGRAPHY OF THE JAREDITE JOURNEY

The Zagros mountain range begins in eastern Turkey and extends to northwestern Iran and roughly follows Iran's western border with Iraq. The mountain range lies to the east of the Tigris River and Mesopotamian Valley. Genesis 8:4 indicates that after the flood, Noah's ark came to rest on dry land upon the mountains of Ararat. Today there is a Mount Ararat located in the Zagros mountain range in Turkey. Although many argue that the modern-day Mount Ararat was not the landing place of the ark, it is generally accepted that the ark did come to rest somewhere along the Zagros mountain range.

In Genesis 11:2 we read that when the land of Babel was established, the people traveled from the east until they came to the plain of Shinar (Hebrew for "land of two rivers"). There they began to build a city and a tower. From this we understand that the people would have traveled westward from the landing place of the ark in the Zagros Mountains to find a land of two rivers (Tigris and Euphrates) where they began to construct the city of Babel. Genesis 10:10 instructs us that Babel was a part of the kingdom of Nimrod, which included the cities of Babel, Calneh, Erech, and Accad, all

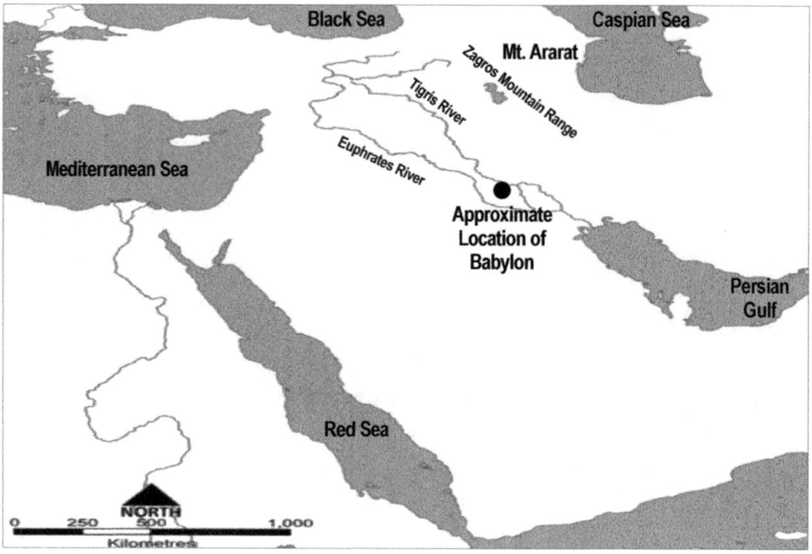

The general region where Babel was constructed

located in the land of Shinar. Historically, most scholars have placed Babel near Babylon. However, recent studies have argued for a more northern location in modern Turkey or Syria closer to the headwaters of the Tigris River and westward of the current Mt. Ararat.[1] Thus, it is possible that the city of Babel may have been located anywhere within the vicinity of the Tigris or Euphrates rivers.

The people of Babel had intended to build a tower of fired brick and bitumen tar. As such they would have needed access to these materials as well as the means to transport them. The use of boats on the Tigris or Euphrates rivers as well as wagons pulled by animals would have been the most obvious methods of transportation of these materials. Similarly, the people of Babel would have developed vessels to transport liquid tar and water to support the construction of the tower. Without these transportation methods, the construction of the tower could not have been undertaken.

Similar transportation methods were also needed in the travels of the Jaredites. We know from the record of the Jaredites that their journey included a significant number of people and supplies. Crossing the wilderness with these people and their provisions would have required a sizable caravan. This caravan would have involved the use of wagons and oxen similar to the wagons needed for construction activities in Babel.[2]

By studying the geography around the land of Babel and comparing it to the geographical information in the scriptures, we can formulate some general thoughts on the travel of the Jaredites. From the scriptural record we discover the following:

- The people migrated from the east to establish the city of Babel (see Genesis 11:2).
- The Jaredites left Babel and traveled northward to the valley of Nimrod (see Ether 2:1).
- From the valley of Nimrod, they traveled into that "quarter where there never had man been" (see Ether 2:5).
- The seashore at the end of the Jaredites' overland journey seemed to be in a moderate climate as the Jaredites dwelt in tents for four years (see Ether 2:14).

As noted above, we know the Jaredites initially traveled to the north of Babel down into the valley of Nimrod.[3] From there, they traveled into that "quarter where there never had man been" (Ether 2:5). Thinking in terms of "quarters" we typically would divide our directions into the northern, southern, eastern, and western quarters. We know that the people had originally migrated from the east to establish the city of Babel, and therefore, the eastern quarter had already been inhabited prior to the time of the Jaredites. The eastern quarter also contained a substantial mountain range that would have been difficult to transverse with a large caravan of people. As such the eastern quarter was an unlikely direction for their travels. The Jaredites initiated their journey by traveling into the valley Nimrod, which was north of Babel. Traveling southward back toward the land of Babel would also be an illogical direction unless they traveled in a round-about way. Continuing a route directly to the north would also seem improbable as it would lead to colder climates and eventually the impassible Arctic Ocean. Because travel in the eastern, northern, and southern quarters was improbable, westward would be the most likely direction of travel for the Jaredites to take. This would have led them across the Arabian Desert, Jordan Valley, or Turkish lands toward the Mediterranean or Red Sea.

The suggested westward direction of travel is not intended to provide definitive answers or doctrinal instruction but is merely a probability analysis based on available information. The Lord often has other ideas and certainly could have led the people through an uninhabited eastern mountain pass or softened the elements of the Arctic Ocean. By faith, the brother of Jared may have even moved the mountains to provide a path of travel for his people (see Ether 12:30). The purpose in including this information is to inform the reader of the history and geography of the area and invite them to ponder the influence that the land had on the Jaredite travels.

NOTES

1. Anne Habermehl provides a case for the Tower of Babel to be located in upper Syria or lower Jordan in the paper "Where in the world is the tower of Babel?" (*Answers Research Journal* 4 [2011]:25–53). See answersingenesis.org/arj/v4/where-tower-babel.pdf. Accessed April 22, 2020.
2. Hugh Nibley noted in his book *The World of the Jaredites* (Salt Lake City: Bookcraft, 1952) that wagons and oxen were available and likely used in the Jaredite Journey.
3. The Book of Mormon notes that the Jaredites assembled "down" in the valley of Nimrod that was northward of Babel. From the map it can be seen that the waters of the Tigris and Euphrates rivers flow southward toward the Persian Gulf. As water will always flow downhill, the elevation must always increase as you travel northward along these rivers. Therefore, it is unlikely that there would be a valley north of a plain, with an elevation below that of plain between the Tigris and Euphrates rivers. Such a valley would fill with water and become a lake, particularly given the recent occurrence of the flood. Some possible explanations may be that the word *down* does not necessarily connote a lower change in elevation. It is also possible that the Valley of Nimrod may not be located between the two rivers. As the brother of Jared had the faith to move the mount Zerin (Ether 12:30), it is also possible that the valley of Nimrod is now a mountain. Assuming that the valley of Nimrod still exists, it would be an interesting geographical study or even a crowdsourcing

study to research locations where a valley is located to the north of a large plain that could fit the description of the "valley of Nimrod" and the "plain of Shinar."

Chapter 7

WERE BARGES BUILT AT AN INLAND SEA?

The Jaredites' travel in the wilderness is documented in three verses found in Ether 2:5–7. These verses provide a summary of the Jaredite travels between the valley of Nimrod and their arrival at the promised land:

> And it came to pass that the Lord did go before them and did talk with them as he stood in a cloud, and gave directions whither they should travel.
>
> And it came to pass that they did travel in the wilderness, and they did build barges in which they did cross many waters, being directed continually by the hand of the Lord.
>
> And the Lord would not suffer that they should stop beyond the sea in the wilderness, but he would that they should come forth even unto the land of promise, which was choice above all other lands which the Lord God had preserved for a righteous people.

There is an ongoing debate of whether the barges noted in verse 6 were the barges used to cross the ocean or if the Jaredites had encountered an inland sea during their travel in the wilderness and built barges prior to arriving at the ocean seashore. This debate continues as there are different ways to interpret Ether 2:6–7. The first interpretation is to assume the words "beyond the sea in the wilderness" in verse 7 indicate that during their travels in the wilderness, the Jaredites encountered an inland sea—with the words "in the wilderness" defining the location of the inland sea. If the Jaredites encountered an inland sea during their journey in the wilderness, they would have needed to build boats or barges to cross it before reaching the ocean seashore. In this interpretation, the barges noted in Ether 2:6 would have been used to traverse the inland sea that they encountered during their journey in the wilderness.

However, there is another way to interpret these verses. It was Moroni who wrote these words as he dwelt in the new or promised land. From his perspective in the new land, the words "beyond the sea" would refer to the other side of the ocean and other hemisphere from where Moroni dwelt. Rather than defining the location of an inland sea, the words "in the wilderness" would have defined the place where the Lord would not permit them to stop—specifically at the ocean seashore in the wilderness. In this interpretation, the barges noted in Ether 2:6 would have been the same barges used to cross the ocean and the term "many waters" specifically meant the ocean.

In the terms of the Jaredite story, the second explanation is the more persuasive for the following reasons:

1. Geographically, there are no inland seas in the area of the Euphrates River that do not have a direct connection to the ocean—with the possible exception of the Caspian Sea. The Caspian Sea, however, is an unlikely candidate for the Jaredites' travels because it would have led them in a northeast direction from the land of Babel toward the Arctic Ocean.
2. We know the Jaredites stopped on the ocean seashore for four years and only resumed their journey after the Lord chastised them. Thus, we know that the Lord did not permit them to remain or stay at the seashore, which is consistent with the second explanation.

3. The Jaredites must have traveled in a large caravan, which likely included wagons and oxen. The logistics of transferring supplies to barges to cross an inland sea and then rebuilding wagons to continue an overland journey on the opposite side of the sea would have been logistically problematic.
4. The term "many waters" used in Ether 2:6 was again used by Moroni to describe the ocean voyage in Ether 6:7. Nephi also used the term "Irreantum" as a name for the ocean, which was interpreted as "many waters" in 1 Nephi 17:5. As such it would have been common among the Nephites to use the term "many waters" to describe the ocean. Thus, the barges used to cross "many waters" in Ether 2:6 would have been consistent with crossing the ocean.
5. When read as a whole, Ether 2:5–7 appears to be a short synopsis of their travel from the valley of Nimrod to the promised land. If Moroni intended these verses to be a synopsis of all of their travels, then it would be illogical to mention barges used to cross an inland sea but not mention the barges used to cross the ocean.

For these reasons, this book will assume that the Jaredites did not encounter an inland sea, and the barges noted in Ether 2:6 are the barges used to cross the ocean. It should be noted that if the Jaredites had encountered an inland sea during their travels, they would not have crossed the inland sea or any other body of water using submersible barges constructed similar to those they used to cross the ocean. The barges used to cross the ocean were unsuitable to sustain life as there was no light or air in them and the people would have perished (see Ether 2:19). We know from the record that the lack of light and air in the ocean crossing barges was not resolved until just prior to the Jaredites' ocean journey. Therefore, any boat, vessel, or barge used during their wilderness travels would not have been constructed similar to, or in scriptural terms, "after the manner of" the ocean-crossing barges.

Although the map of the general area does not include a large inland sea, it is probable that the Jaredites had to cross the Euphrates River or other smaller bodies of water during their wilderness travels. When they came to these obstacles, the obvious choice would have been to construct a ferry-type boat to transfer flocks, people, wagons, and beasts across the water. Given the Jaredites' proficiency at planning their journey and building vessels noted previously, constructing a ferry or similar type of boat to cross a smaller body of water would not have been difficult for them.

Although uncertainties exist regarding the direction and obstacles the Jaredites encountered in their wilderness journey, it must have been a marvelous and faith-building experience for the Jaredites to be led by the Lord and hear His voice as He talked with them from the cloud and gave them direction where they should travel. No matter where the Jaredites traveled or how the Jaredites arrived at the ocean seashore, we know that Jared, his brother, and their people were faithful in following the Lord's directions. These people were fulfilling their most cherished desire to obtain their promised land and were continually led by the hand of the Lord as they crossed the wilderness to the seashore.

Chapter 8

FOUR YEARS ON THE SEASHORE

The Jaredites were led by the Lord out of Babel, through the wilderness, and to a distant ocean seashore. Once at the seashore, Moroni's abridgement condensed four years of the record down to one single verse: "It came to pass that the Lord did bring Jared and his brethren forth even to that great sea which divideth the lands. And as they came to the sea they pitched their tents; and they called the name of the place Moriancumer; and they dwelt in tents, and dwelt in tents upon the seashore for the space of four years" (Ether 2:13).

It would seem that Moroni did not give us enough information in this one verse to develop an understanding of what occurred during the Jaredites' initial four years on the seashore. However, if we wish to develop some theories or conclusions of what likely happened during this time, we must start by assembling the information that we do know, rather than dwelling on the unknown. By considering the facts we do have, we may find that the four years the Jaredites spent on the seashore were instrumental in developing the character and faith of the Jaredites.

What do we know about the people in this story? What can we learn from an analysis of their character? What would these people have done upon their arrival at the seashore? During the preparations in Babel and the journey to the ocean seashore, we gain specific insights into the character of Jared, the brother of Jared, and the Jaredites, as well as the Lord's relationship with these people. These character analyses help us understand what actions they may have taken upon their arrival at the seashore:

1. JARED: We know Jared was a faithful man who put a great deal of trust in his brother and recognized him as his spiritual leader. Ether 1:38 in particular describes the faithfulness, diligence, and determination of Jared as he talked to his brother and sought to obtain the promised land: "And who knoweth but the Lord will carry us forth into a land which is choice above all the earth? And if it so be, let us be faithful unto the Lord that we may receive it for our inheritance."
2. THE BROTHER OF JARED: We know the brother of Jared was the spiritual leader of the people and that he had received revelation and direction to lead the people to the seashore. The Lord Himself recognized the prayerful nature of the brother of Jared while answering his prayer in Ether 1:43: "There shall be none greater than the nation which I will raise up unto me of thy seed upon all the face of the earth. And thus I will do unto thee *because of this long time ye have cried unto me*" (emphasis added).
3. THE PEOPLE OF JARED: We know these were people of great ingenuity who had sufficient faith to avoid the confounding of their language and the vision to follow a prophet of God into the wilderness. These were people who, when united in their goal to obtain the promised land, could do anything "which they imagined to do."
4. THE LORD: We know that the Lord had answered the prayers of the brother of Jared and had blessed the Jaredites and led them in every step they took from Babel to the seashore. Ether 2:6 specifically records that the

> people of Jared were "directed continually by the hand of the Lord."

Given what we know about these people and the Lord who led them, it would seem out of character for these people to forget their goal and do nothing for four years upon reaching the seashore. Would the brother of Jared who had cried unto the Lord for a "long time" to receive the direction that led them to the seashore have immediately abandoned his prayers upon reaching the sea? Would the Lord have ceased giving direction although He had "continually" led the people by his hand? Lastly, would Jared and his people have quickly abandoned their quest to attain the promised land just after reaching the seashore? From what we know of these characters, this seems highly unlikely.

Based on their history and character, the Jaredite people would have rejoiced at reaching a major milestone of their journey but then would have wanted to continue their quest for the promised land. Upon arrival at the seashore, these intelligent people would have realized that there were only two possibilities:

1. The seashore was in fact the promised land.
2. The promised land was on the other side of the sea and the only known way to cross the sea was by ship.

Moroni gives us a definitive indication that these people knew soon after they arrived at the seashore that the seashore was not the promised land and was not their final destination. In fact Moroni says three times that "they pitched their ***tents*** . . . and they dwelt in ***tents***, and dwelt in ***tents*** upon the seashore for the space of four years" (Ether 2:13; emphasis added).

The people of Jared were formerly city dwelling people from the land of Babel. If these people thought they had reached their final destination, would they have dwelt in tents? If there were resources to build boats, there were also resources to build dwellings. If the Jaredites thought the seashore was the promised land, why didn't they build dwellings or houses? The only logical answer is that the people knew from the day they reached the seashore that the seashore was not their final home. If the Lord led the people to the seashore, and the people knew that the seashore was not their final destination, they must have also realized the only direction they could go was to cross the sea. The only way to cross the sea was with a ship or boats.[1] Therefore, it can be concluded that from the time they reached the seashore the Jaredites knew they had not reached their final destination. They knew they needed to build boats or a ship to cross the ocean.

NOTE

1. Regarding the definition of ships, boats, and barges, the difference between a ship and a boat is generally understood to be the size of the vessel with a ship being much larger than a boat. Thus, it would take several boats to equal the capacity of one ship. It is interesting, however, that the Book of Mormon would use the word *barge* to describe the vessels built by the brother of Jared rather than a ship or a boat.

   It is possible that during the translation process there was some differentiation in the mind of Joseph Smith between a ship, a boat, and a barge. From Doctrine and Covenants 1:24 we know that the Book of Mormon was translated by Joseph Smith "after the manner of (his) language." Joseph Smith would have been familiar with barges commonly used on the Erie Canal near to his home in Palmyra. Thus, the word *barge* was likely identifiable to him as something different than a typical boat or a ship. Barges used on the canal were likely of the same approximate size as the barges used by the Jaredites, as Ether 2:17 indicates that they were the "length of a tree." Additionally, the barges on the Erie Canal were not self-propelled or self-steered, but were driven and steered by horse or oxen pulling from the side of the canal. The barges built by the brother of Jared were also not self-propelled or self-steered, which is unlike a ship or boat that would be driven by a sail, rudder, or oars. As such, Joseph may have identified the vessels to be similar to a barge. Barges today, however, are not submersible. As we consider the Jaredite barges today, we would probably identify them as some type of rudimentary submarine, which was unknown during Joseph Smith's time.

   I use the words *ship* or *boats* in some places because the Jaredites would have initially thought they would build a conventional ship or multiple boats to cross the ocean. However, as the brother of Jared received the instructions from the Lord, the Jaredites realized that these vessels were not conventional boats or ships. Thus, they likely came up with a new name for them similar to the way we differentiate between ships, boats, barges, and submarines. In Joseph Smith's language the name the Jaredites used was likely translated to the word *barge*, as it may have been the best description Joseph was familiar with in his time and language.

Clark Goble in his writing "Some Thoughts on Jaredite Barges" (*Times and Seasons*, https://www.timesandseasons.org/harchive/2017/02/some-thoughts-on-jaredites-barges/index.html) addressed Joseph Smith's use of the word "barge" and noted similarities between the barges built by the brother of Jared and the barges used on the Erie Canal.

Chapter 9
THE SEASHORE THEORY: PART ONE

In the previous chapter, we determined that upon their arrival at the seashore, the people of Jared had been faithful in every command given by the Lord and were determined to reach the promised land. Furthermore, it was concluded that the Jaredites must have known that the promised land was on the other side of the ocean, and the only way to cross the ocean and reach the promised land was by ship or boats. We also evaluated the character of the people such that we know the Jaredites were faithful and the brother of Jared had prayed unceasingly for direction. Because of these prayers, the Lord had given direction continually.

Given the character and disposition of the Jaredites, it is likely that upon reaching the seashore they knew they needed to build a ship to cross the ocean. Subsequently, the brother of Jared would have sought the instruction of the Lord just as he had always done. Whenever the brother of Jared inquired of the Lord, the Lord continued to give direction. If the Lord gave direction to the brother of Jared upon their arrival at the seashore, He certainly didn't direct them to sunbathe on the seashore for the next four years. The obvious instructions from the Lord would have been to prepare for the next segment of the journey and build barges to provide a way to cross the ocean.

Upon receiving instructions to build the barges, the Jaredites would have pitched their tents and then commenced building the barges, reflecting their determination to continue on their quest to the promised land.

Therefore, for the purposes of this book we will hypothesize that the Lord directed the people of Jared to build barges, and they commenced building barges as soon as they reached the ocean seashore. This hypothesis is different from most scholarly interpretations of the story of the brother of Jared. Many assume that because the book recorded no events during the four years on the seashore that nothing significant occurred during this time. However, a careful reading will reveal that nowhere in Ether 2 does it specify *when* the Lord gave the brother of Jared the plans to build these unusual barges, only that the barges were built "according to the instructions of the Lord." This hypothesis is based on analysis of the disposition of the Jaredite people and the desire of the Lord to "continually" direct His people. We can analytically test this hypothesis by comparing it with other evidence in the record of the Jaredites' journey. We can spiritually test this hypothesis by evaluating the known spiritual events that follow and determine if they are spiritually compatible with the proposed hypothesis.

Given that these events are thousands of years old and that the information is limited, we must also concede that there is no way to prove this hypothesis or any other hypothesis presented in this book. As such the findings of this book can only be labeled a theory. For the purposes of this book, we will call this collection of hypotheses the "Seashore Theory." The Seashore Theory will provide a basis to obtain potential answers for many of the unanswered questions found in the story of the brother of Jared.

The first hypothesis of the Seashore Theory is therefore as follows: The Lord gave instructions and a plan to build the barges. The Jaredites commenced building the barges when they initially arrived at the ocean seashore.

To test this hypothesis of the Seashore Theory, we will evaluate known events or outcomes that occurred during or after the initial four years the Jaredites spent on the seashore. We can then evaluate what events would have resulted in the known outcomes. From the record, what events can we determine occurred during or after their four years on the seashore? From Ether 2:14 we can conclude that during the four years on the seashore, the brother of Jared became complacent in his prayers: "At the end of four years . . . the Lord came again unto the brother of Jared . . . and for the space of three hours did the Lord talk with the brother of Jared and chastened him because he remembered not to call upon the name of the Lord" (Ether 2:14).

This scripture does not specify when the brother of Jared ceased to pray, or the length of time the brother of Jared had faltered in his prayers. However, given the three-hour chastisement, it would appear that the brother of Jared had been less than faithful in his duties for a long time, most likely years. Furthermore, we do not know if the brother of Jared ceased praying entirely or became complacent and unfeeling in his prayers. Regardless of this, we know that his efforts, or lack thereof, were unacceptable to the Lord.

After chastising the brother of Jared for his lack of prayer, the Lord then addressed the subject of the barges: "And the Lord said: Go to work and build after the manner of barges which ye have hitherto built" (Ether 2:16).

The Lord's use of the word *hitherto* in Ether 2:16 indicates that the people of Jared had built barges before. Where else would the Jaredites have built barges after this "manner"? Some people have theorized that they built barges in Babel or at an inland sea in the wilderness.[1] However, the record clearly defines the "manner" of barges that were built as being "tight like a dish" and lacking light and air (Ether 2:17–19). In short, barges built after this "manner" were unusable. If the barges were unusable, then we know that barges such as this were not used in Babel nor in the wilderness. The only place the Jaredites would have "hitherto" built barges after this "manner" and not subsequently used them would have been during the Jaredites' initial four years on the seashore as hypothesized.[2]

The Cambridge online dictionary[3] defines the word *hitherto* as "up until now." As such the Lord's use of the word indicates that the Jaredites "up until now" had been building barges after a specific manner or plan. If the Jaredites had been building barges up until now, what had made them stop? If the people had been faithfully working to build barges, then why would the Lord tell the people to "go to work and build"? If the brother of Jared had not been faithful in his prayers, then perhaps the people of Jared had also been less than faithful in building barges per the direction of the Lord. This brings us to the second hypothesis of the Seashore Theory: During the four-year time period on the seashore, the brother of Jared faltered in his prayers. The people of Jared likewise faltered in their assignment to build the barges and eventually abandoned the effort. Given these hypotheses of the Seashore Theory derived thus far, two specific questions emerge:

1. Why would the brother of Jared, who had hitherto been so faithful in offering prayer to the Lord have faltered and abandoned his prayers?
2. Why would the Jaredites, who had hitherto been so faithful in following the Lord's directions, have faltered and abandoned the Lord's direction to build the barges?

It appears something must have happened during the Jaredites four years on the seashore that inhibited their spiritual and physical progress toward their goal of obtaining the promised land.

NOTES

1. Other theories regarding where the Jaredites had "hitherto" built barges center around the interpretation that the Jaredites had encountered an inland sea and had constructed barges to cross the inland sea as noted previously in chapter 6 of this book. These theories fail to address the "manner" portion of the Lord's directive.
2. Hugh Nibley interpreted the phrase "as ye have hitherto built" to mean barges or ships that mankind had previously built, specifically referring to Noah's ark. Justification for this interpretation was based on Ether 6:7 where the barges were noted to have similarities

to the ark. See *The World of the Jaredites* (Salt Lake City: Bookcraft, 1952) and Nibley's *An Approach to the Book of Mormon* (Provo, UT: Foundation for Ancient Research and Mormon Study, 2015), in the collection of Nibley's works.

3. See dictionary.cambridge.org/us/dictionary/english/hitherto.

Chapter 10

THE SEASHORE THEORY: PART TWO

In 2013, I had successfully constructed my first home and purchased a piece of land to begin construction on a second. As I surveyed the property, I realized that the land was large enough to build a home that was fifty percent larger than the first home I had built. From the onset I knew that I did not have the funds to complete the larger home that I had designed, but I estimated that by doing more of the work myself I could save money to make up the difference. My miscalculation became apparent as I ran out of needed funds before I was able to complete all of the interior finishes. In my mind I could hear the words of the Savior: "Which of you, intending to build a tower, sitteth not down first, and counteth the cost, whether he have sufficient to finish it? Lest haply after he hath laid the foundation and is not able to finish it, all that behold it begin to mock him" (Luke 14: 28–30).

I had started the construction of a home but failed to count all of the costs. After much effort, I eventually found lenders willing to loan the funds I needed to complete the home. I had initially planned to keep and occupy the home, but with the added debt, I found myself in a position where I needed to sell the home to repay the money I had borrowed. I learned the importance of careful planning, designing, and "counting the costs."

"Counting the costs" entails much more than a financial analysis. It would make little sense to build a tower that was not tall enough to see over the trees, that was not strong enough to withstand the wind, or that was not durable enough to last for many years. Failure to count the costs of functionality and durability would bring as much mockery as failing to finish the tower in the first place.

As demonstrated by the Lord's parable of the tower, the principles of careful planning, designing, and counting costs have been observed since the beginning of time. The people of Babel had meticulously planned the Tower of Babel prior to beginning construction. We know this because the intent of the people of Babel to build a tower was specifically stated and the materials and methods that builders intended to use were individually mentioned in the Bible. The Lord Himself said the people of Babel were capable of doing anything that they "imagined," or in other words, designed and planned to do. The one cost the people of Babel failed to consider in building their tower was the cost of angering God.

Planning and designing are a collaborative and repetitive process requiring input from owners, designing architects, engineers, manufacturers, suppliers, contractors, and financiers. Creating a design can often take longer than the time needed to build a structure or manufacture a piece of equipment. Generally, a model or prototype is constructed as part of the planning process to help ensure that functional and durability costs have been considered. The model or prototype is used to identify and correct any deficiencies prior to building the actual project or before putting a product into full manufacturing.

Having come from Babel, the Jaredite people were intimately familiar with design, manufacturing, and construction protocol. Their detailed preparation for their journey into the wilderness indicated that these people were meticulous planners who knew how to "count the costs" prior to embarking on an endeavor. Upon reaching the seashore they immediately knew that they needed to build a ship or boats so they could reach the promised land. If the Lord had simply commanded them to design and build a ship to cross the ocean, the Jaredites likely had the experience and background necessary to have done it. However, the Lord had a different plan.

The barges envisioned by the Lord came with a very specific plan or "manner" that was highly unusual and different from any boat that had previously been built. These barges were "tight like a dish" and "peaked at the ends." When the door was shut it was also tight so that when the barges were swallowed in the depths of the ocean, they would be tight and submersible even as a "whale in the midst of the sea" (Ether 2:17; 24).

Not only were the barges unusual, but the instructions that the people received from the brother of Jared were also different from typical design and construction protocol. What design process had been followed? Who had counted the costs? Who had designed the barges?

The brother of Jared would have presented the plans for the barges to the people, but the profession of the brother of Jared was likely that of a priest or a shepherd, and as such he probably had the least construction experience. Of all the people in the Jaredite party, he was likely the least qualified to provide instructions for the barges. How would the people know the barges would work and that the plans actually came from the Lord? Given the Jaredites' construction background, they would have built a prototype so they could see how the barges would function and ensure the costs had been counted.

It is also possible that the plans for the barges were not all given at one time. When Nephi built his ship, he recorded that "the Lord did show me from time to time after what manner I should work the timbers of the ship" (1 Nephi 18:1). If the brother of Jared received his instructions in a similar manner, the people may not have known what the barges were going to look like, or how they would operate until the first barge was nearly complete.

Following typical construction protocol, the Jaredites would have expected that the first barge would serve as a prototype to evaluate its functionality. What would they have learned while building the first barge? Surely before the first boat was completed, these intelligent people noticed that the barge had no air, no light, and no way to steer. The prototype was useless. What fool among them was going to volunteer to test the prototype and demonstrate its capability on the open ocean? What financier or manufacturer among them would have been willing to back the construction of the next seven units?

Given the Jaredites' construction background, problem solving capability, and propensity to meticulously plan, how did they react when they realized the prototype barge they built was incomplete at best and deadly at worst? To the Jaredites it would have appeared that the functionality costs had not been fully counted.

Upon finding these defects there was surely some contention among the Jaredites. Some of the Jaredites may have fractured the unity of the group and criticized the wisdom of the brother of Jared for asking them to build such a useless vessel. Others may have presented their own solutions to modify the Lord's plan. Some may have wanted to design and construct a more conventional ship, and others may have decided to not participate in the work until all the contention and problems were resolved.

From Noah to Nephi we know that building a ship to comply with the commands of the Lord is not an easy task. Nephi in particular struggled to convince his wayward brothers that building a ship was possible. Laman and Lemuel rebelled when their help was needed the most. Exasperated with the indifference of his brothers, Nephi admonished them: "If the Lord has such great power and has wrought so many mighty miracles among the children of men, how is it that he cannot instruct me that I should build a ship?" (1 Nephi 17:51).

Even though Nephi was building a conventional ship that had a sail, could be steered, and stayed on the surface of the water, he struggled to convince his family that the instructions came from the Lord and would result in a seaworthy ship.

Given the experiences of Nephi, we can assume that the brother of Jared may have struggled to maintain the unity of his people. Unlike Nephi, he may have had some doubts himself regarding the seaworthiness of the barges. Similar to Laman and Lemuel, the Jaredites may have complained about the difficulty of the task and mocked the brother of Jared for the glaring defects in the plans. Seeing this division among his people, the brother of Jared possibly spent a good amount of time chastening and admonishing them in hopes of restoring their unity. These people would have wanted answers to their legitimate questions before continuing on an obviously useless endeavor. The brother of Jared may also have wanted answers as to why the Lord gave him incomplete plans and placed him in this predicament with his followers. The pride of the people in their own intelligence and in their own ingenuity may have prevented them from continuing the effort to build the barges in the Lord's way.

Given the prayerful nature of the brother of Jared, we can assume that he decided to enter the nearby mountain to pray and request the Lord provide the missing pieces of the plan. If he knew how the Lord would provide light, air, and a way to steer, then he could convince the people—and possibly himself—that the Lord really did have a purpose in this plan. However, the plan of the Lord was never really about the barges. The plan of the Lord was to prepare His people for the promised land. As such, it would appear that the Lord's intent was to use the barges to teach the Jaredites to repent, become united, and trust and serve Him as their God. The Lord would try their faith before giving them further directions.

Unlike the previous times the brother of Jared had approached the Lord, there would be no answers and no explanation. The only direction the Lord would give the brother of Jared would be the quiet whisper of the Spirit to repent, trust the Lord, and complete the task they were assigned to do. However, the Jaredites were too fixated on the immediate deficiencies to see the wisdom of the overall plan. Unlike every other question the brother of Jared had hitherto brought before the Lord, direction could not be obtained by prayer alone. As such, it would seem that the brother of Jared returned from his prayers without the answers he expected. The defects in the barges still remained and no clarification from the Lord was forthcoming. In exasperation with the apparent indifference of the Lord, the brother of Jared may have thought to himself: "If the Lord has such great power and has wrought so many mighty miracles among the children of men, how it is that he cannot instruct me that I should build a ship?"

When it became clear the barges were useless and the Lord was not going to give the desired answers, would the people of Jared have abandoned their efforts to build the barges? Did they become complacent on their comfortable seashore? Perhaps the people questioned the inspiration and calling of the brother of Jared. Would they have considered the brother of Jared to be a fallen prophet? Would the brother of Jared have become discouraged if he wasn't receiving the answers he expected? In his discouragement would he have found it difficult to pray with honesty or real intent? Would he have stopped praying all together?

If these are the events that occurred, the people of Jared may have thought the designer of the barges didn't know how to build barges or ships at all. If he did, why would the plans not address these three critical defects? How could God fail to count the costs? Furthermore, why did the Lord, who had answered every question and led every step in the wilderness, suddenly become unavailable? If the barges were clearly useless, and the Lord was no longer answering their questions, then why should they continue to build and pray?

Based on the known outcomes, the character of the people, and the certain difficulty they experienced when building the barges, we can assess why the brother of Jared faltered in his prayers and why the people abandoned the construction. Given these possible events in combination with the hypotheses of the Seashore Theory noted previously, we can develop additional hypotheses to answer these questions. Specifically, the next three hypotheses of the Seashore Theory include the following:

1. The brother of Jared and the Jaredites were highly intelligent people who quickly recognized the deficiencies in the barges prior to the first one being completed.
2. The brother of Jared requested the Lord provide answers to the apparent defects in the barges early in the process, but the Lord chose not to answer as a trial of the Jaredites' faith.

3. The apparent defects in the Lord's design of the barges and the lack of additional direction from the Lord contributed to the people abandoning the construction of the barges and the brother of Jared's faltering in his prayers.

The difficulty with the barges may not have been the only reason the Jaredites and their prophet struggled on the seashore. We know by our own experience that life is not easy, and even the righteous are not exempt from deep trials. On the contrary, many of the Lord's most chosen servants have experienced debilitating illness, loss, and pain. Many righteous people have lost precious loved ones or even children to disease or accident. Others have experienced the depths of depression or the depravity of oppression.

While the experiences and trials of Jared, his brother, and the people on the seashore are not recorded, each of us know and have experienced sorrow and trials that are part of life. As such, it is probable that the Jaredites experienced sickness, loss, or other trials of their faith during this time. It often takes time to come to terms with our trials and realign our hearts to accept the will of the Lord. It might even take four years.

The last hypothesis of the Seashore Theory is therefore: The Jaredites may have experienced sickness, loss, or other trials of their faith during the four years on the seashore which also contributed to their separation from the Lord.

SUMMARY OF THE SEASHORE THEORY

During the Jaredites' initial four years on the seashore, it is hypothesized that the following events occurred:

1. The Lord gave instruction and a plan to build the barges, and the people of Jared commenced building the barges when they first arrived at the seashore.
2. During the four-year time period on the seashore, the brother of Jared faltered in his prayers. The people of

Jared likewise faltered in their assignment to build the barges and eventually abandoned the effort.

3. The brother of Jared and the Jaredites were highly intelligent people who quickly recognized the deficiencies in the barges prior to the first one being completed.
4. The brother of Jared requested that the Lord provide the answers to the apparent defects in the barges early in the process, but the Lord chose not to answer as a trial of the Jaredites faith.
5. The apparent defects in the Lord's design of the barges and the lack of additional direction from the Lord contributed to the people abandoning the construction of the barges and the brother of Jared's faltering in his prayers.
6. The Jaredites may have experienced sickness, loss, or other trials of their faith during the four years on the seashore that also contributed to their separation from the Lord.

Chapter 11

PREPARING THE PEOPLE FOR THE PROMISED LAND

A casual reading of the story of the brother of Jared would indicate that neither the brother of Jared nor the God who led him were aware of the flaws in the barges until after all eight of the barges were built.

With this simplistic reading it would appear that Deity had no capacity to design barges and the Jaredites were equally incompetent at building them. It would seem that Jared, his brother, and all the Jaredite people were so incapable they did not realize there was no light inside the barge after they built the first one. Subsequently they boldly built seven more defective barges before the town genius entered the eighth barge and said, "Wait a minute, it's dark in here. There is no light! Quick, go check the other barges!"

The premises of an incompetent God and bumbling builders would seem to be the exaggerated plot for a slapstick comedy, if we did not know the architect of the barges was the Lord Jesus Christ and the builder was His chosen prophet. Surely the Lord Jesus Christ who created the heavens and the earth knows the minor details of ship building. As such the only possible conclusion is that the Lord knew and understood from the beginning the instructions He gave the brother of Jared were incomplete and contained the three flaws.

Because the Lord is perfect, it can further be concluded that the three defects in the barge design were intentional and an integral part of the Lord's plan to prepare His people to enter the promised land.

In Ether 2:8–12 Moroni gives a dissertation on the blessings of the promised land and the righteousness needed for a people to obtain and dwell within it. From these verses we learn the following:

- The promised land is a choice land above all other lands.
- Whosoever possesses the promised land shall be free.
- The inhabitants of the promised land must repent.
- The inhabitants must serve the God of this land who is Jesus Christ.
- Those who fail to serve God until they are "ripened in iniquity" will be swept off.

Moroni himself was intimately familiar with the failures of the Nephites to serve the Lord and retain their place in the promised land. He witnessed firsthand as the Nephites ripened in iniquity and were swept off of the face of the land because they failed to repent and serve God.

Preparing a people for the promised land seems to be a theme in many of the stories of the Lord's people. The people of Moses wandered in the wilderness for forty years as the Lord prepared them to enter the promised land. Likewise, it seems the four years of time spent on the seashore were also necessary to prepare the hearts of the Jaredite people for their journey. Indeed, the Lord's only work and goal is to prepare His people to enter the true promised land and return to His presence: "For behold, this is my work, and my Glory, to bring to pass the immortality and eternal life of man" (Moses 1:39).

The Lord prepares the hearts of His children for the promised land by virtue of their own experiences. The Lord ensures that each of us has the experiences we need to know good from evil that we may learn to choose the good and become like Him. Like the wanderings of the people of Moses in the wilderness, or the stumblings of the people of Jared on the seashore, we learn and grow from our struggles and choices. These experiences give us the humility, moral education, and spiritual preparation we can obtain no other way.

Indeed, it is the Lord's plan for us to come to earth and stumble in our journey that we may taste, know, and experience the evil, and by so doing appreciate, love, and desire the good. The necessity of this education is so great that our loving Father in Heaven prepared the Atonement of Jesus Christ so we could learn this essential knowledge and still have a way to repent and be saved from our sins.

As such, sin is not the delineator that divides the evil souls from the good but the educator that teaches us the difference. The true delineator of an evil and good person is not sin but repentance and faith in the Lord Jesus Christ. Moroni teaches us that repentance is the key to obtaining the promised land and that we must repent and serve God rather than "ripen in our iniquities" (Ether 2:9). Likewise, the true "promised land," the celestial kingdom, will be full of those who in their past have committed every kind of sin that would otherwise eternally doom our souls into outer darkness if not for repentance and the Atonement of Jesus Christ. It is faith in Jesus Christ and repentance through His Atonement that defines a celestial being—not lack of sin. The only sin that can truly keep us out of the celestial kingdom is our refusal to repent.

When the Lord chastened the brother of Jared for failing to pray and chastised the Jaredites for failing to repent, He said:"But thou shalt not sin anymore, for ye shall remember that my Spirit will not always strive with man; wherefore, if ye will sin until ye are fully ripe ye shall be cut off from the presence of the Lord" (Ether 2:15).

When we recognize our state of sin, Satan would have us believe that our souls are lost. It is the Holy Spirit that constantly leads us back through repentance and prayer. If we cease to pray and refuse to repent, then we are denying the promptings of the Holy Ghost. Continuing to deny the direction of the Holy Ghost and refusing to repent can eventually become a sin that is unpardonable that will cut us off from the presence of the Lord (see Alma 39:6).

Therefore, our daily prayers are the front line in the battle for our eternal souls. No matter how many times we falter, we are not lost if we continue to obey the Holy Spirit and approach our Father in humble prayer. Our personal prayers are the delineator between whether we are repenting or whether we are denying the promptings of the Holy Ghost who teaches us that we "must pray always" (2 Nephi 32:8–9).

During their initial four years on the seashore, the Jaredites likely made mistakes and committed many types of sins. However, the Lord was most concerned about their failure to pray and refusal to repent. These are the sins that deny and separate us from the Spirit and eventually cut us off from the presence of the Lord. Thus, a lack of prayer and refusing to repent are the sins that would have denied the Jaredites the promised land and can likewise deny us eternal life with our Father.

Chapter 12

GO TO WORK AND BUILD

The Seashore Theory states that upon their arrival at the seashore, the Jaredites began construction of the barges according to the Lord's command but soon abandoned the effort. The Jaredites subsequently spent four years waiting on the seashore, expecting a more perfect plan to appear. These people of intellect knew better than to build barges with no light and no air. They had been given the Lord's plan but had judged the barges to be defective and not worthy of their effort unless all their questions were answered. However, during these four years, no better plan emerged and no answers came.

Once the Jaredites were humbled by their failures and lack of progress, the Lord again approached the brother of Jared: "And it came to pass that at the end of four years that the Lord came again unto the brother of Jared and stood in a cloud and talked with him. And for the space of three hours did the Lord talk with the brother of Jared and chastened him because he remembered not to call upon the name of the Lord" (Ether 2:14).

Oftentimes, the scriptures do not record the spiritual trials and personal struggles of the prophets. Yet, we know the brother of Jared experienced an extended period where his prayers, or lack thereof, were not acceptable to the Savior. In the Church today, some may have labeled the brother of Jared as "fallen away" or "inactive."

Knowing the struggles and failings of the brother of Jared makes his experiences more relatable and shows us no matter our perception of our relationship with the Lord, He is not out of reach.

As the brother of Jared repented and prayed in behalf of his brethren, the Lord directed his attention to the barges: "Go to work and build barges, after the manner which you have hitherto built . . . according to the instructions of the Lord" (Ether 2:16).

At this time, the brother of Jared likely asked the Lord about the deficiencies in the barges that he was directed to build. Once again there would be no answers coming from the Lord regarding the lack of light or air in the barges. The commandment to "go to work and build" would be all the direction he would receive. In this encounter, the brother of Jared came to understand the Jaredite people would have to build the barges by relying on faith that the Lord would eventually provide answers.

After the Lord chastened the brother of Jared for failing in his prayers and chastised the people for failing to build the barges, the brother of Jared had a difficult task; he had to repent and call his people to repentance. He had to restart the barge building project with renewed determination despite the known defects. Furthermore, he had to convince Jared and the people to repent and assist in the effort of building the barges despite the lack of answers. The brother of Jared had no explanation to his fellow brethren other than to say, "I do not know why the barges have no light, or how the Lord will eventually provide air. I don't know if we will even be able to use these barges, but I *know* this is the work the Lord commanded us to do." The people would learn the barges had to be built by testimony and faith more than by labor and sweat.

More important than the building of the barges was the preparation of the people. By love, persuasion, and testimony the brother of Jared rekindled the desires of the people and united their hearts in the goal of constructing the vessels. He convinced them to "go to work" like the Lord commanded. From their experience at the tower, the brother of Jared knew a united people could accomplish anything that "they imagined to do," but a people united in the work of the Lord would receive miracles from Him that would exceed anything they could imagine. Indeed, it would require multiple miracles for these barges to become seaworthy.

As the people repented and began building the barges, the brother of Jared likewise repented of his failure to pray. His prayers, however, must have changed. Where previously he complained of the lack of light in the barges, he prayed for increased faith and spiritual light. Praying for daily physical strength to build became more important than worrying over lack of physical air in the future journey. Concerns regarding steering the barges were set aside as he prayed for guidance on how to direct and lead his people. By uniting his people in the construction of the barges, the Jaredites would see that allowing the Lord to steer their lives was imminently more productive than the aimless direction of the previous four years.

As the construction of the barges progressed, the faith of the people grew. Each tree that fell, each board that was cut, each nail that was placed was an act of faith. Each of these physical actions was done with a worldly certainty that the effort was meaningless but a heavenly faith that the Lord would not require they labor in vain. With each testimony borne by the brother of Jared that the work was the will of the Lord, a drop of lasting faith was added to the brother of Jared's reservoir. Likewise, by acting on that testimony and by laboring and constructing the barges, the people also built the faith they needed to become worthy of the promised land. Day after day, month after month, year after year, each small and simple act of building useless barges was part of the Lord's great and magnificent plan to build obedient faith.

An all-knowing Lord designed "defects" in the barges from the beginning so that these simple, daily acts of building faith would change a non-praying and inactive man into a great and faithful prophet. Likewise, the Lord used these small acts of building faith to prepare the hearts of the Jaredites to obtain the promised land.

Chapter 13

THE PHYSICAL NATURE OF FAITH

In early summer of 1977, I walked out of the Broadway Theater in downtown Salt Lake City with a new goal in life—to be a Jedi Knight when I grew up. The latest blockbuster movie had left a definite impression on me. I wanted to learn how to use the powers of "the force" to move and control the material objects around me. However, years of swinging a plastic lightsaber never yielded the desired result of being able to control external matter using the mind. I would never become a Jedi Master.

Later in life the words of the Creation became significant to me as I read these words in Abraham: "And there stood one among them that was like unto God, and he said unto those who were with him: we will go down, for there is space there, and we will take of these materials and we will make an earth whereon these may dwell" (Abraham 3:24).

We know that the one who "was like unto God" was the great creator, Jesus Christ. He created the earth by using the power of the priesthood to command and organize matter. We also know that Michael the Archangel and other faithful spirits who were with him in the premortal world participated in the creation of this earth by the power of the priesthood. When commands were given in the name of Jesus

Christ the matter obeyed, forming mountains, oceans, streams, trees, vegetation, and all varieties of animals.

As I realized this, I wondered if perhaps I had been one who was with Christ in the premortal life and had participated in some way in the creation of the earth. While the Lord Jesus Christ created and moved mountains, perhaps I was able to command and move pebbles. When the Lord created the oceans, perhaps I had the opportunity to create puddles. Participating in the Creation in even a small way would have been a wondrous privilege. The work that was accomplished in creating this glorious earth and giving it life far exceeded the powers of any mythical Jedi Knight.

The ability to command and control external matter by the power of the priesthood may have been one of the stages of our eternal development that we learned and experienced in the premortal world. Participation in the creation of the earth may have been our master's thesis in that stage of our learning. But our Father in Heaven had an even greater vision of our eternal progress.

In order to become like our Father, we needed to do more than just command and control external matter. We would have to clothe our spirits in flesh and become one with the matter. We would have to train our spirits to overcome and control carnal matter from the inside rather than merely command obedient matter from the outside. The body and the spirit together would become a living soul. Furthermore, the matter and the spirit would no longer be subject to the commands of God, but this living soul would be given its own agency and freedom to choose. Our souls would have the freedom to choose the desires of the flesh or the will of the spirit. This precious gift of agency was given to us to determine whether the natural man would win control over our spirits or if our spirits could subdue and tame the natural flesh. This is the ongoing struggle of this earth.

The interaction of our bodies and spirits are an integral role of our Heavenly Father's plan for our progression. In order for us to regain His presence, our spirits must subdue the will of the flesh. This is done by incremental and repetitive action wherein the determination of the spirit learns to overcome the desires of the flesh.

The spirit of a newborn baby has little or no control over his body. His arms and legs may flail about incessantly with no direction. Over time the spirit placed in this tiny body begins to control the motions of the fleshy matter that surrounds it. The tiny baby learns to control the eyes, arms, hands, legs, and feet as muscles become subject to the spirit. The child and the parents both rejoice in each small step as the spirit of the child gradually learns to move and control the body that encompasses it. Through the repetitive, mundane movements, muscle memory becomes built into the body such that the spirit can command it to run, jump, climb, throw, or any number of other physical activities, and the matter obeys. Over time and with repetitive motions, the spirit can train the body such that people become talented musicians, accomplished artists, or great athletes. In others, the spirit may engage the mind to become great thinkers or accomplished teachers.

Faith is likewise built using repetitive, mundane acts of submitting our soul to the will of God. The story of the brother of Jared is an amazing record of a man who progressed from a state of inactive faith to standing in the presence of God. But how was this accomplished? What were the steps the brother of Jared made that brought about this incredible change of heart? What changed the Jaredites from being a content and idle people on the seashore to a people of great faith who witnessed miracles and obtained the promised land? The answer appears to lie in the mundane, repetitive physical acts of building the barges. Elder Juan Pablo Villar said, "Just as reading and learning about muscles is not enough to build muscle, reading and learning about faith without action is insufficient to build faith."[1]

When Adam was cast out of the Garden of Eden, he was informed that "by the sweat of thy face shalt thou eat bread" (Genesis 3:19). Far from being a curse, this was a blessing by which he and all of us, as his posterity, could show and develop our faith. In the instance of the brother of Jared, that work was building the barges by "the sweat of his face," despite the worldly evidence that the barges were dysfunctional. The commandment from the Lord to "go to work and build barges" was really a command to go to work and build faith. The brother of Jared would awake every day and testify to his family that despite the obvious and unanswered flaws, building the barges was the work of the Lord. Then he would set the example by laboring with his might to build the flawed vessels. Each physical action of cutting a tree or driving a nail was an act of spiritual muscle memory where his body and soul were trained in acts of obedient faith. This repeated physical action demanded that his mind and his flesh learn submission to the will of God.

Like physical muscle memory, spiritual muscle memory is obtained by exercise, or more specifically, exercising our faith. This spiritual muscle memory is obtained by submitting our physical bodies and our eternal soul to the work of building the kingdom of God. Thus, exercising our faith is best accomplished by physical acts that discipline our physical body and soul according to the will of God. While we know the work of our hands cannot bring salvation, the work of our hands can subdue the natural man and increase our faith in Him who has the power to save.

NOTE

1. Juan Pablo Villar, "Exercising our Spiritual Muscles," *Ensign*, May 2019.

Chapter 14

MAKING WEAK THINGS STRONG

In 2004 my bishop called me to be the Primary chorister. My immediate reply was, "I'm a guy. Isn't this a better calling for my wife?" I had never considered or wanted this assignment, but I had been taught to never turn down a calling. Initially I resisted the calling and just stood before the children waving my arm in a less than musical pattern and singing with even less enthusiasm. I had no previous experience teaching music to children and felt weak and incapable in the calling.

After a few weeks the Primary president asked me to teach the children the song "Scripture Power." After reviewing the words, my wife recommended that I use some of my creative construction skills to make a sword, shield, helmet, and other armor to accompany the second verse. I subsequently made the silliest looking armor ever and the kids loved it. I found that the way to be successful in my calling was to have fun and make a fool of myself in front of the kids each week. This was something I seemed especially adept at. Furthermore, I loved singing songs that inspired me as much as they inspired the children. Through music and word, I had the opportunity to bear my testimony of the gospel. I loved it. I loved the children. I had fun in the calling, and the children had fun too.

The assignment I originally perceived to be a weakness became a source of joy and an opportunity to bless children. In this calling I developed skills and found gifts that I did not know I had. The Lord had taken a weakness in me and turned it into a strength. The calling of Primary chorister has been my favorite assignment.

During their initial time on the seashore, the Jaredites also discovered that their assignment was a stumbling block. The lack of light and air in barges prevented them and their prophet from accomplishing their desired goals. The lack of answers to these defects was perceived by the people and their prophet as a weakness in the Lord's plan. However, in reality those defects exposed a weakness in the faith of the people themselves—a weakness that would have to be overcome before they could obtain the promised land.

After four years and some chastisement by the Lord, the brother of Jared repented, restarted the construction project, and testified to his people of the importance of building the barges. Upon receiving his testimony, Jared and his brethren also went to work. Becoming united in the effort through testimony and faith, the people were able to accomplish the construction of eight unusable, but spiritually fulfilling, barges.

Upon completing all eight barges according to the Lord's plan, the brother of Jared was finally able to return to the Lord and report that the required work had been done. In Ether 2:18 we read: "And it came to pass that the brother of Jared cried unto the Lord saying: O Lord, I have performed the work which thou hast commanded me, and I have made the barges according as thou hast directed me."

It is interesting to see that *before* the brother of Jared asks for instruction on how to obtain light, air, and the ability to steer, he takes the time to report to the Lord that the work is complete and he has made all eight barges. He also reports that all of the barges have been constructed according to the directions of the Lord—including the obvious flaws and defects. This preface to his prayer is an indication that the brother of Jared had addressed these questions previously with the Lord but had come to understand that the work must be complete according to the Lord's plan before the answers would come.

When the brother of Jared had previously requested answers to these questions, the Lord's answer was simply "go to work and build." Until that time, it was not necessary for him or the people to know the answers to these questions in order to build the barges. In fact, it was necessary that he and his people *did not* know the answers to these questions so they could build their faith. By reporting to the Lord that the work was complete and that the barges had been built according to the Lord's plan, the brother of Jared and his people had demonstrated their faith. They were now prepared to receive the answers to the three issues: "And behold, O Lord, in them is no light; wither shall we steer? And also we shall perish, for in them we cannot breathe, save it is the air which is in them; therefore we shall perish" (Ether 2:19).

With the completion of the work, the Lord saw that the brother of Jared had increased his faith through his labor as the Lord intended. The brother of Jared was now prepared to receive the next instruction for the barges, which would further increase his faith. The next step of the Lord's plan was to answer the three concerns of the brother of Jared in three separate ways:

1. There is no air: The Lord gave specific directions to the brother of Jared where to cut holes in the barges to provide air. The brother of Jared had to act on these directions (see Ether 2:20).[1, 2]
2. There is no light: The Lord asked the brother of Jared to ponder the problem, come up with a solution, and return and present his solution to Him (see Ether 2:25).
3. There is no way to steer: The Lord addressed this issue by asking the people to trust Him to be their pilot and guide. He then sent a furious wind to blow the barges towards the promised land (see Ether 6:5).

When we pray for answers, the answer the Lord gives to our prayers may consist of very similar directions:

- The Lord may ask us to prepare ourselves by going to work and building our faith in spite of unanswered questions.

- The Lord may provide an answer, but it is up to us to act in order to accomplish the provided solution.
- The Lord may ask us to ponder and choose a solution to be presented to the Lord.
- The Lord may ask us to place our trust in Him to provide for our needs.

While the Lord answered the brother of Jared's prayers in four different ways, it should also be noted that the answers came at four different times. No answer was given to the next step until the previous direction was completed. All eight barges had to be completed according to the Lord's instructions before the Lord gave directions to provide the barges with air. Once the Jaredites had cut the holes and provided the barges with air according to His instructions, the brother of Jared was prepared for the next step to provide them with light. Likewise, the Lord did not send the wind to steer the barges until after the shining stones were in place and giving light to the vessels.

Each successive answer was designed and intended by the Lord to require an increasing amount of faith and preparation. When the brother of Jared accomplished the directive, the Lord provided a corresponding degree of reassuring knowledge that their faith and action had not been in vain. The directive to cut the holes for air assured the people that the Lord understood the need for air and had planned for it from the beginning. The miracle of the shining stones gave the people evidence and knowledge that God was surely with them on their journey. This evidence gave the people the faith necessary to enter into a barge that could not be steered and embark into an endless ocean. After this demonstration of their faith, the Lord solved their final dilemma by steering their barges across the ocean to the promised land.

Jared and his people originally came to the Lord with one desire and one question: How could they obtain the promised land? We know there is only one way to attain it—through faith in the Lord Jesus Christ. The Jaredites needed to increase their faith in order to be worthy of their desired goal. The three intentional flaws in the barges initially exposed the weakness in the Jaredites' faith. However, when the people humbled themselves, repented, and learned to trust in the Lord's plan, the Lord was able to use the flaws to strengthen their faith and prepare their hearts. Thus, the defects that originally exposed the weakness in the faith of the Jaredites became the key that the Lord used to strengthen their faith so they could obtain the promised land.

> And if men come unto me I will show unto them their weakness. I give unto men weakness that they may be humble; and my grace is sufficient for all men that humble themselves before me; for if they humble themselves before me, and have faith in me, then will I make weak things become strong unto them. (Ether 12:27)

NOTES

1. It is commonly asked why the Lord waited until the barges were constructed before directing the Jaredites to cut a hole in the top and a hole in the bottom. Why not install the hole during construction? The Lord wanted to test and build the Jaredites' faith. However, there may be engineering answers as well. Stress distribution around a hole functions best if a round hole is cut in a uniform material. The hull of the barges were likely constructed using timbers laminated and sealed together. Allowing the timbers to bind and seal together creating a more uniform material prior to cutting a round hole would provide for optimal stress distribution around the hole. This assumes the barges were made of wood—which the record does not specify except to say they were the "length of a tree" (Ether 2:17).
2. Why did the Lord direct them to cut a hole in the top and the bottom of the barge? Ventilation is only functional if there is cross ventilation with openings on two opposing sides of the barge. The hole in the "bottom" may not have been placed directly in the lowest part of the barge, but likely just above the water line in calmer waters. It is also possible that the bottom hole was pressurized using a bellows or other methods. Hugh Nibley also mentions the possibility of pressurizing the holes or possibly pressurizing an air tank to provide air when the barges were submersed (Nibley, *An Approach to the Book of Mormon*, 344).

Chapter 15

THE TOUCH OF THE MASTER'S HAND

The Tower of Babel was the greatest building project in the history of the earth at the time the construction was commenced. In order to build the tower, the leaders had assembled the best architects, engineers, contractors, material suppliers, and financiers. The plans had been prepared to the best ability of mankind. Through their knowledge and labors, they were sure they would enter the realms of the heavens. Years of labor and countless costs had been expended to build this world wonder, and yet, with one command from the mouth of God, it was all for naught. Despite the great and grand designs of men, the tower was never finished. The work was left incomplete.

In contrast to the great tower that would reach above the clouds, the Jaredites were directed to construct barges that would descend below the waves. The people exercised their faith and labored to construct the vessels according to the plans, but an essential element of the barges was missing. The barges had no light. There was no known way to provide light within the vessels. Yet, without that light, all of their efforts in traversing the wilderness and constructing the barges would be for naught.

The Lord asked the brother of Jared what he would have Him do to prepare light for the barges while crossing the sea. In a day when we have LED, incandescent, and fluorescent light bulbs we may not think about the dilemma this placed upon the brother of Jared. What sources of light had he experienced? The sun, the moon, and the stars were the most obvious source of light available to the earth. Fire certainly would have given light but would have consumed the oxygen in the barges. Other sources of light may have included lightning, sparks, or natural sources such as fireflies. However, there was no way to capture, maintain, or sustain these light sources. Given the limitations of these sources of light, the brother of Jared had no options.

In considering these sources of light, there may have been one other source of light that intrigued the brother of Jared. As the brother of Jared conversed with the Lord through the cloud, there must have been light emanating from the presence of the Lord. Like Moses saw in the burning bush, the light from the Lord would have been constant and did not consume fuel. Furthermore, this light was likely different from fire or other manufactured light. The light from the cloud would have been as the light from the sun—giving life to those who viewed and absorbed it. This is the only light he would have been familiar with that could have provided the light and life needed within the barges as they descended into the oceans. Without this light, all of the work on the barges would have been for naught. However, the only way to obtain or borrow this light would have been to go to the source and humbly ask for it:

> Now behold, O Lord, and do not be angry with thy servant because of his weakness before thee; for we know that thou art holy and dwellest in the heavens, and that we are unworthy before thee; because of the fall our natures have become evil continually; nevertheless, O Lord, thou hast given us a commandment that we must call upon thee, that from thee we may receive according to our desires.
>
> Behold, O Lord, thou hast smitten us because of our iniquity, and hast driven us forth, and for these many years we have been in the wilderness; nevertheless, thou hast been merciful unto us. O Lord, look upon me in pity, and turn away thine anger from

> this thy people, and suffer not that they shall go forth across this raging deep in darkness; but behold these things which I have molten out of the rock.
>
> And I know, O Lord, that thou hast all power, and can do whatsoever thou wilt for the benefit of man; therefore touch these stones, O Lord, with thy finger, and prepare them that they may shine forth in darkness; and they shall shine forth unto us in the vessels which we have prepared, that we may have light while we shall cross the sea. . .
>
> And it came to pass that when the brother of Jared had said these words, behold, the Lord stretched forth his hand and touched the stones one by one with his finger. (Ether 3:2–6)

When the Lord reached out and touched the stones prepared by the brother of Jared, they burst forth with the light of Christ implanted in them by His touch. Radiating with light, the stones were placed within the heart of the vessels, giving light and life to the people and validating the faith of their efforts. With the touch of the Lord, years of labor in building the barges were redeemed from becoming a thing of naught. The barges were transformed into vessels of salvation that could carry the people to the promised land.

In each of our lives, we expend great efforts. Sometimes our efforts are impressive and gain notoriety throughout the world. More often our greatest struggles occur within the walls of our own home or within the chambers of our own heart. Whether we expend our lives in leading nations or struggling within our souls, at some point we realize that all of our efforts cannot bring us into the realm of heaven. We may refine and shape our stony heart in an attempt to make it clear and void of impurities, but we cannot infuse it with the light we need to fill our soul.

Each of us must prepare ourselves and humbly approach the Lord and implore Him to extend His hand beyond the veil and touch our soul that our heart may be filled with His light. It is only His touch and blessing that can sanctify our faith and labors as a vessel for our salvation. It is only His touch that can redeem our souls and fill us with His light that we may complete our journey to the promised land.

Chapter 16

THE PERFECT PLAN

Critics of the Book of Mormon have noted the story of the brother of Jared as evidence that the Book of Mormon is not true. Specifically, they have claimed that God would certainly know how to build barges and would not design plans that did not account for light and air. However, we know the Lord wasn't building barges; the Lord was building faith.

The Lord's work is to "bring to pass the immortality and eternal life of man" (Moses 1:39). If this is the Lord's work, then it is likely His plan as well. If we consider the story of the brother of Jared from the Lord's perspective, His plan included having the brother of Jared develop his faith by building barges that were useless to the understanding of man. Each of the three flaws were in place for a reason to help him increase his faith and bring him closer to the Savior. We can see that the Lord's plan to bring to pass the salvation of the brother of Jared was indeed intricate and successful:

> And the Lord saw that the brother of Jared had fallen to the earth, and the Lord said unto him: Arise, why hast thou fallen?
>
> And he saith unto the Lord: I saw the finger of the Lord and I feared...
>
> And the Lord said unto him: Because of thy faith, thou has seen that I shall take upon me flesh and blood; and never has man come

> before me with such exceeding faith as thou hast; for were it not so ye could not have seen my finger. Sawest thou more than this?
>
> And he answered: Nay Lord show thyself unto me.
>
> And when he had said these words, behold, the Lord showed himself unto him, and said: Because thou knowest these things ye are redeemed from the fall; therefore ye are brought back into my presence. (Ether 3:7–13)

Thus we see that the Lord's plan successfully redeemed the brother of Jared and brought him into His presence. If the Lord's specific plan for the brother of Jared was successful, one may ask, when did the Lord formulate this plan? Was it when the brother of Jared made the stones, built the barges, or left Babel?

Our all-knowing and all-loving Father in Heaven formulated the plan of salvation before the foundation of this world. In that plan, we would leave our premortal state, come to earth to receive a body, and learn to exercise faith in our Savior, Jesus Christ. Jesus Christ, the central figure in this plan, would take upon Him our sins so that we could repent and return to our Father's presence. We often portray the plan of salvation as a simplified diagram as shown:

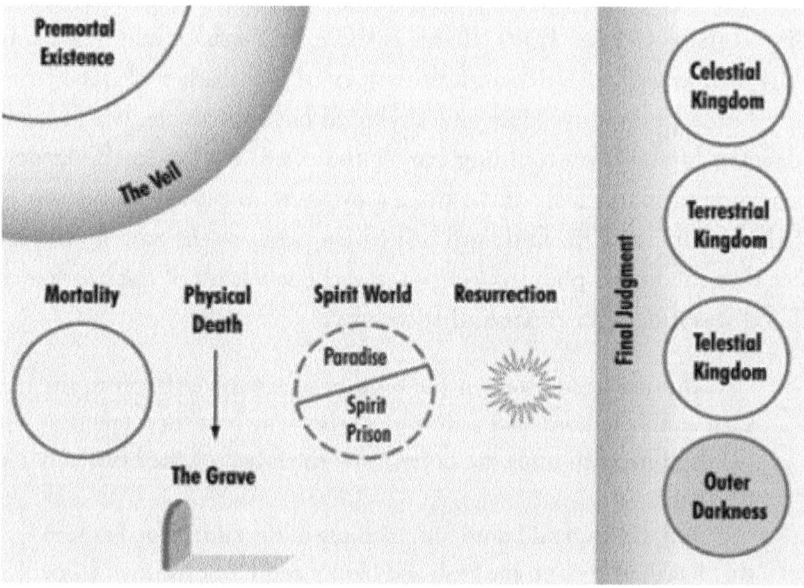

The plan of salvation as shown on ChurchofJesusChrist.org

The knowledge we have gained of the great plan of salvation through the revelations to the Prophet Joseph Smith have greatly increased our knowledge of the purpose of life and our eternal destiny. Yet, it would seem that the Lord's plan to bring the brother of Jared back into His presence was much more intricate and detailed. If the Lord has such an intricate plan for each one of us, then the diagram we use to represent the plan of salvation is merely the banner that hangs over the doorway to an immense library containing countless volumes of plans for the salvation of each of our souls.

Our all-knowing Father in Heaven knew the mind and heart of the brother of Jared to the extent that the Lord was able to develop a perfect plan for his individual salvation. The Lord knew and planned that the act of constructing the barges would add to his faith in a manner that would prepare him to stand in His presence. Each of the flaws in the design were specifically intended to increase his understanding and trust in the Lord. When the Lord requested that the brother of Jared come up with his own solution to provide light within the barges, the Lord already knew the outcome. The departure from Babel, the travel in the wilderness, the time on the seashore, the barges, and the stones were all part of the Lord's perfect plan to use imperfect barges to redeem an imperfect man.

If the purpose of life was to be a test to determine the eternal destination of the earth's occupants, the brother of Jared would likely have failed while he sojourned on the seashore. But the Lord had a greater vision for the potential of the brother of Jared. Where we envision a test, the Lord envisions a classroom. The Lord designed the specific obstacles and trials the brother of Jared needed to progress from his inactive and dormant state to becoming worthy to enter into the presence of the Lord.

When the Jaredites started building the first barge, they surely noticed the flaws in the design. It is likely the brother of Jared fasted, prayed, and pleaded with the Lord for the answers he thought were necessary to finish the assigned task. Yet, if the Lord had given the answers at the beginning, it would have removed the necessary lessons, hampered the progress of the people, and kept the brother of Jared from obtaining the faith he needed to enter the presence of God. As such *not answering* the prayer of the brother of Jared in the way he desired was an essential part of the Lord's plan and an essential part of the brother of Jared's salvation.

If the Lord had such an intricate and personal plan to provide for the salvation of one man, then it stands to reason that He has an intricate personal plan for the salvation of each of us. Likewise, when we plead for answers but feel that heaven is closed, it is not because the Lord does not have the answers we seek, but instead, the Lord has the perfect plan to bring about the salvation of our souls. If the Lord were to answer all of our prayers and remove all of our obstacles, it would negate His perfect eternal plan to bring each of us back into His presence.

Chapter 17

ULTIMATE FAITH

The people of Babel were the scientific and political leaders of the world in their day. They had knowledge unrivaled throughout the world, and like our day they had the capacity to do anything they imagined. However, Satan put it into their hearts to use their knowledge and abilities for the most audacious of all scientific endeavors—to discover God, to uncloak Him from His hiding place, and intrude upon Him in His heavens. Like the militant atheists of our day, the people of Babel believed their ability to discover God was greater than God's ability to conceal Himself. Their pride was so exalted they considered their own ability equal to or greater than God.

From the people of Babel we learn that God's knowledge and power is much greater than the imaginations of mankind. With one decree from the mouth of God, the tower and mankind's feeble attempts to disprove God's existence were brought to naught, and the knowledge and capacity of Babel were scattered.

From the story of Babel, we learn that God's capacity to conceal Himself always exceeds man's capacity to discover God. It would seem there is no way man could find God, uncloak Him from His hiding place, and enter unbidden into His presence. If this is the lesson learned from Babel, then what contrasting lesson do we learn from the brother of Jared?

When the brother of Jared saw the finger of the Lord, the Lord Jesus Christ showed Himself unto the brother of Jared. The Lord then informed him of the following: "And never have I showed myself unto man whom I have created for never has man believed in me as thou hast" (Ether 3:15).

With all the great prophets who existed before the Jaredites, this statement would seem unlikely. Surely Adam, Enoch, Noah, and others also had great faith, saw God, and entered into His presence. Why would the Lord tell the brother of Jared, "Never have I showed myself unto man"? Elder Holland explored this question in depth in his book *Christ and the New Covenant*. After presenting several explanations he proposes:

> A final explanation—and in terms of the brother of Jared's faith the most persuasive one—is that Christ was saying to the brother of Jared, "never have I showed myself unto man in this manner, without my volition, driven solely by the faith of the beholder." As a rule, prophets are invited into the presence of the Lord, are bidden to enter his presence by him and only with his sanction. The brother of Jared, on the other hand seems to have thrust himself through the veil, not as an unwelcome guest, but perhaps technically as an uninvited one. Said Jehovah, "Never has man come before me with such exceeding faith as thou hast; for were it not so ye could not have seen my finger. . . . Never has man believed in me as thou hast." Obviously, the Lord himself was linking unprecedented faith with this unprecedented vision. If the vision itself was not unique, then it had to be the faith and how the vision was obtained that was so unparalleled. The only way that faith could be so remarkable was its ability to take the prophet, uninvited, where others had been able to go only with God's bidding.[1]

The prideful people of Babel had so rudely determined they would be the ones to force themselves uninvited into Gods presence. The Lord, in contrast, showed it is not only possible to enter God's presence, but with exceeding faith it is even possible for man to enter His presence without invitation. The Lord saw this potential in the brother of Jared. The Lord knew he had the faith and humility necessary to enter the presence of the Lord uninvited and unbidden. Through humble faith, rather than audacious pride, the brother of Jared would accomplish the exact intent of the people of Babel.

Moroni expounds further on the exceeding faith of the brother of Jared in Ether 3:19–20:

> And because of the knowledge of this man he could not be kept from beholding within the veil and he saw the finger of Jesus . . . and he had faith no longer for he knew nothing doubting.
>
> Wherefore, having this perfect knowledge of God, he could not be kept from within the veil; therefore he saw Jesus; and he did minister unto him.

The brother of Jared's faith was such that he "could not be kept from beholding within the veil." It would seem that because of his exceeding humility and great faith, the brother of Jared's ability to see God did in fact exceed God's intent to conceal Himself. Therefore, he saw Jesus, and He did minister unto him.

The ministering of Jesus to the brother of Jared was an unparalleled experience as the Lord Jesus Christ showed him all things and told him to write it in a language that He had confounded. Just as the Lord had confounded the languages of the people of Babel to keep them from discovering His secrets, the Lord revealed all of His secrets to the brother of Jared but recorded it in a confounded language. The Lord had obviously known from the very beginning that the brother of Jared would be the one to see, experience, and write this important work. In short, even though the brother of Jared may have entered unbidden into the presence of the Lord, he had not entered into His presence unknowingly or unwelcomed. The manner in which the brother of Jared would enter the Lord's presence and the vision which he would behold had been foreordained by the Lord since before the beginning of Babel.

NOTE

1. Jeffrey R. Holland, *Christ and the New Covenant* (Salt Lake City: Deseret Book, 1997), 23.

Chapter 18

THE VISION OF MANKIND

The brother of Jared climbed the mountain, entered the heavens, and found the living God. He witnessed the finger of the Lord, and the record notes that "having this perfect knowledge of God, he could not be kept from within the veil; therefore he saw Jesus." Having entered the presence of the Lord, Jesus then "showed unto the brother of Jared all the inhabitants of the earth which had been, and also all that would be; and he withheld them not from his sight, even unto the ends of the earth" (Ether 3:25).

When Jesus showed the brother of Jared all the people who would live on the earth, he would have seen people who would build huge skyscrapers far taller than the Tower of Babel. He would have come to know people who would discover and develop flight that would carry people above the tops of the tallest buildings. He would have even seen people who would invent, design, build, and travel in rockets that would go to unimaginable heights and leave the gravitational orbit of the earth.

In addition to seeing these people who would soar to such great heights, he would see people who would design and build nuclear submarines that would generate their own light and oxygen. He would see people in these submarines who could travel around the entire earth without the need to come above the water's surface.

The brother of Jared would have seen people who attained the greatest heights of space and the greatest depths of the ocean. He would have learned that the Lord Jesus understood and knew all of the advanced technology that would take mankind to these great extremes, and that lighting and steering the barges paled in comparison to God's matchless knowledge and power. In spite of all the miraculous technology and advancements mankind would attain, these advancements would bring mankind no closer to entering into the realm of the heavens and the knowledge of God than the futile attempts of the ancient people of Babel.

The vision of mankind would demonstrate to the brother of Jared, and to us, that infinitely more important than the technology and advancements of mankind were the people themselves. The vision would show that Jesus Christ knows and loves each of the inhabitants of the earth personally. The value of each of His children is greater than the value of any technology or physical creation, for the world was created for the salvation of the Lord's children.

Of all the earth's inhabitants, the most important was the Lord Jesus Christ Himself. The brother of Jared saw that Christ would descend from His heavenly throne, walk upon the surface of the earth, suffer, bleed, and die for the sins of the world, and rise from the grave to bring salvation to mankind.

We must also understand that when Jesus Christ showed the brother of Jared all the inhabitants of the earth, he surely saw each of us. He saw that the Lord Jesus Christ knows who we are and knows how to bring salvation to us if we are willing to develop a personal relationship with Him.

If the brother of Jared, as a prophet of the Lord, saw and knew each of us in his vision of mankind, then surely the Lord Jesus Christ saw and knew each of us personally when He walked the earth. In Isaiah's vision of the Messiah he recorded that when the Lord Jesus Christ made His soul an offering for sin, He would "see his seed" (Isaiah 53:10). Abinadi expounded on this statement and defined "his seed" as all of us who had learned His word and believed on His name (see Mosiah 15:10–11). From this we know Christ saw and knew each of us as He took upon Him our sorrows and sins in the Garden of Gethsemane.

The Apostles who witnessed Christ's prayer in the Garden of Gethsemane bore record of His intense and infinite suffering as He took upon Him the sins and pains of this world. It was Luke who recorded the words of the Savior in Gethsemane when He pleaded with His Father to "remove this cup from me" but in obedience accepted the Father's plan with the words "not my will, but thine be done" (Luke 22:42).

In His suffering, Luke recorded, there "appeared an angel unto him from heaven, strengthening him. And being in agony he prayed more earnestly: and his sweat was as it were great drops of blood falling down to the ground" (Luke 22:43–44). It is worth pondering how a mere angel could possibly strengthen Jesus Christ—for Jesus Christ Himself was God, having power, strength, and resolve that exceeded that of any multitude of angels. The answer perhaps is within Isaiah's prophecy.

Within our mortal understanding, the comfort Christ could have obtained in His agony was to know that His suffering and sacrifice was not in vain but would bring salvation to each of us who believed on His name. As Isaiah said, when His soul was made an offering for sin, He saw His seed. He saw each of us individually. He saw and knew that we had placed our entire faith in Him and without Him and His Atonement, we have no hope. As He saw and knew of our faith in Him, it was His own overwhelming love for each of us that may have strengthened Him in His agony.

Thus, it would seem that faith is indeed one of the most powerful forces in the universe as it was a vision of our individual and collective faith that comforted Christ in the Garden of Gethsemane. Likewise, it was the Savior's love for us and His faith in us to accept His sacrifice that strengthened Him when He took upon Himself our bitter cup.

Chapter 19

FROM THE TALLEST MOUNTAIN TO THE DEEPEST OCEAN

The brother of Jared came down from the mount with the stones prepared by the Lord as well as the knowledge of eternity. Both the issues of air and light in the barges had been resolved. However, there was still one outstanding problem that the Lord had not addressed—"Wither shall we steer?" (Ether 2:16).

It is interesting that several pages of scripture are devoted to resolving the issues of light and air. Yet after Ether 2:16, there is no more mention of the need to steer the ship. It would seem that the brother of Jared and the people of Jared came to understand that there would be no way for them to steer the ship. Of all the difficulties with the barges, this one must have been the most daunting. In order to attain the promised land, the people would have to enter a barge that couldn't be steered and embark into an endless ocean.

When did the people and the prophet come to realize that entering such a barge to cross an endless ocean was the Lord's intent? Was it when the Lord touched the stones? When the barges were finished? Perhaps the people of Jared suspected this from the time they saw the initial plans and were alarmed by the thought.

Prayer can be difficult when we seek the Lord's direction but don't receive answers as we expect them. The lack of expected answers may have contributed to the brother of Jared's difficulty in his prayers. However, there is another possibility. Sometimes it is even more difficult to pray when we know the direction the Lord will give but are not prepared to exercise the faith necessary to follow through with the answers. When the Jaredites initially realized the barges had no steering mechanism, they may have been hesitant to build such a vessel for fear the Lord would actually ask them to risk their lives and use it. Likewise, the brother of Jared may have been hesitant to ask the Lord regarding the steering because he was afraid of the answer the Lord might give.[1]

Asking the Jaredites to enter a barge that couldn't be steered and embark into an endless ocean, trusting their lives to an unseen God, is comparable to a prophet asking his people to jump off a cliff so that God can teach them to fly. In some ways, the prospect of the barge is worse, for if the prophet is wrong, death in a barge would come slowly over years on an endless ocean—not in seconds at the bottom of a cliff.

Having come from Babel, the Jaredites would have known false prophets and corrupt leaders who claimed divine guidance. These false prophets had no aversion to risking or even taking the lives of their people to accomplish their personal goals. Perhaps the brother of Jared was hesitant to be a prophet who told his followers, "We are all going to jump off this cliff together." Perhaps he feared his people would not follow.

What kind of faith and what kind of evidence would be required to convince the people to put their own lives at risk in order to obtain the promised land? What kind of faith and what kind of evidence would be required to convince the brother of Jared to be the leader who risked the lives of every one of his followers?

The Lord Jesus Christ has the capacity to still the storm and calm the waves, but more often the Lord prepares and strengthens His people to withstand the waves and face the storm. In Ether 2:25 the Lord makes it clear that it was His intention to prepare the Jaredites "against the waves of the sea and the winds which have gone forth."

The Lord prepared His prophet and His people by first building their faith by requiring them to build barges. At first the people may have felt like the Lord was requiring them to build their own coffin. However, through the pure testimony of the brother of Jared, the people went to work and increased their faith by constructing the barges. As such, they completed the assigned task and built all eight vessels knowing they were not seaworthy and even dangerous.

Upon completion of the barges, would the increased faith of the people have been enough to convince them to put their lives at risk and leave their comfortable seashore? It would seem the Jaredites needed additional tangible evidence to prepare them for the journey ahead. The Lord knew this as well. The stones that the brother of Jared carried down the mountain were prepared not only for light but for evidence to the people that the hand of the Lord was physically with them on their journey. The light of Christ emanating from the stones was the evidence needed to convince the people to enter the "barges and set forth into the sea, commending themselves unto the Lord their God" (Ether 6:4). The shining stones would have literally been the rock the people relied on for reassurance as they crossed the sea.

Crossing the sea was the critical element of the Jaredite journey as the sea was in fact the gate to the promised land. The leaders of Babel had originally promised the Jaredites that their city would be the gate of God. Nephi, however, explained that the true gate to the kingdom of heaven is repentance and baptism by immersion (see 2 Nephi 31:17). Like baptism, the Jaredites would descend below the depths of the sea and be immersed in the water as they passed through the "gate" on their journey to the promised land. Likewise, it was the Lord who brought them back on top of the water to receive their new life in their new land. Like the gift of the Holy Ghost, the shining stones given to them by Christ Himself provided the guidance and reassurance for the Jaredites to "commend themselves to the Lord" (Ether 6:4) complete their journey, and obtain the promised land.

NOTE

1. Book of Mormon Central's "How Were Jonah and the Brother of Jared Able to Find Comfort?" has a very interesting discussion that notes many similarities between the prayer of Jonah (Jonah 2:2–10) and the prayer of the brother of Jared in Ether 3:1–2 (https://knowhy.bookofmormoncentral.org/knowhy/how-were-jonah-and-the-brother-of-jared-able-to-find-comfort). The theory presented here that the brother of Jared was hesitant to follow the Lord's command to build unseaworthy barges could also be another connection to the record of Jonah who was hesitant to follow the Lord's direction to preach to the people of Nineveh.

Chapter 20

THE SALVATION OF THE JAREDITES

About twenty years ago, I had a dream in which I received a letter requesting that I meet with President Hinckley on a certain date in his office. In my dream, I put on my best suit and entered the Church Administration Building near Temple Square. Waiting outside the prophet's office, I pondered on the possible reasons that I could have been called there. Was I to have some great calling or responsibility?

When I entered President Hinckley's office and sat across from him at his desk, he gave me a personal priesthood interview, asking about my service and family. At the conclusion of the interview he looked at me as only a prophet could. His look said to me, "I know who you are, and I know what you are capable of doing." He then said, "The gifts of the Spirit are many, and some people are given great leadership capability." He paused for a moment before he added, "But you are just not one of them." He then told me in his great love that I had a strong testimony and that I would have many opportunities to serve and strengthen the Church but that he didn't see me serving in a bishopric or stake presidency. He instructed me to be a leader in my home and accept the callings that I was given to serve in the Church. If I did these things, I could fulfill the work the Lord had for me to do.

When I awoke from my dream, I was not sure if I had received a message from the Lord or direction from my inner psyche. Regardless, the analysis seemed to be correct as the personal spiritual gifts I had been given seemed to be more specific to creativity and teaching, rather than leading and delegating. Since I had that dream, I have found great joy in my opportunities to serve as a Primary chorister, Primary teacher, elder's quorum instructor, Sunday School counselor, and temple worker. Although I know the Lord has the capacity to turn weaknesses into strengths, I do not expect I will serve as a leader like the brother of Jared.

The story of the brother of Jared gives us a detailed account of how the Lord meticulously laid out a plan to bring about his salvation. But what about Jared and his people? Were they just the Lord's pawns to bring about the salvation of one spiritual giant? Was the Lord as concerned about the individual people of the Jaredites as He was about their spiritual leader?

Jared and his people were faithful followers of the Lord. From the time the Lord began to confound the languages of the people of Babel, Jared recognized the hand of the Lord in confounding the languages and scattering the people. Furthermore, Jared recognized the spiritual gifts of his brother and knew that he was "highly favored of the Lord" (Ether 1:34). Thus, Jared and his brother had a spiritual background and history that extended well before the time that the Lord began to confound the languages of the people. It is also likely that the friends selected by Jared and his brother where chosen not only because of their relationship but because Jared and his brother had a spiritual history with them as well. They knew their friends would be faithful to the Lord so that all might obtain the promised land.

Several of the friends of Jared and his brother were likely chosen because they had skills and resources necessary to prepare for and embark on the extraordinary journey. These skills would have included construction, designing, engineering, hunting, farming, beekeeping, and fishing. There were also likely planners, financiers, accountants, suppliers, guides, and outfitters required to embark on the journey. Each person had a talent or a gift to contribute to this expedition that Jared and his brother could not have accomplished alone. Without these people, this physical and spiritual journey would not have been possible.

The Lord has said there are many gifts of the spirit and that the Lord gives them to people according to his will, one to one and one to another. We are instructed to "deny not the gifts of God" (Moroni 10: 8–19). Each of the Jaredite people were needed in this physical and spiritual journey, and their accomplishments were attributable to their combined efforts. To deny the contributions or efforts of any one of the people would be equivalent to denying the gifts of the Spirit granted individually to people by God.

Even the fact that we know the prophet by the title "the brother of Jared" is a testament that he knew the work and faith of his brother Jared, and his people were equally important to the Lord as were his own extraordinary accomplishments. He recognized the faith and efforts of his brother and their people by choosing to be known by the same name as his brother Jared and the Jaredite people. Unlike the prideful leaders in Babel, he was truly a humble leader who sought to honor his people by making their name and their accomplishments known above his own.

While we know less about the personal experiences of Jared and his people than we know about the brother of Jared, it is worth discussing how the Lord had a plan for their salvation as well. The people of Jared went to work to build the barges just as the brother of Jared asked them to. It is likely they fell away from the Lord during the four-year period on the seashore, just as the brother of Jared drifted spiritually from his calling as their leader. It would have taken greater faith for the Jaredite people to recommence building the barges than for the brother of Jared, because the people did not receive a direct audible witness from the Lord. Yet the scriptures record that "Jared did go to work, and also his brethren" (Ether 2:16). Each board they cut and nail they drove was an act of faith that they performed based on the testimony of their prophet and leader. In order for the people of Jared to make it to the promised land, their faith needed to be strengthened in a similar manner to the brother of Jared. Like the brother of Jared, this was done by acting in faith and building eight barges according to the testimony of their prophet.

The brother of Jared gained his salvation when he moltened the stones out of rock and presented them before the Lord. Likewise, the people of Jared received their salvation or inheritance in the promised land when they saw the stones and "got aboard of their vessels or barges and set forth into the sea, commending themselves unto the Lord their God" (Ether 6:4). Through these acts, the people were able to develop their faith in the Lord to the point they were willing to put their lives into His hands in order to obtain their salvation in the promised land.

While the stories of the individual people of Jared are less dramatic than the record of the brother of Jared, the Lord, nevertheless, knew each one of them and had a plan for their individual salvation. This plan included God-given spiritual gifts that they each used to contribute to the journey. Their individual contributions increased their faith and committed their souls that they also obtained eternal life and exaltation in the promised land according to His plan.

Chapter 21

RENAMING A NATION

In Ether 2:13 it is noted that when the Jaredites first arrived at the seashore, the people "called the name of the place Moriancumer." In the footnote to this verse Alma 8:7 is referenced: "Now it was the custom of the people of Nephi to call their lands and their cities, and their villages, yea even their small villages, after the name of him who first possessed them."

This custom of the people of Nephi was fairly common throughout many cultures and was likely the custom of the Jaredites as well. Because of revelation given to Joseph Smith, we know the actual name of the brother of Jared to be Mahonri Moriancumer. As such, it is interesting to note that the people named their village at the seashore Moriancumer rather than Jared or the Village of Jared. What does this tell us about who the people perceived to be their leader? The naming of their seashore village Moriancumer is an indication the people considered Mahonri Moriancumer to be their leader, and more than likely these people considered themselves the people of Mahonri.

If the people on the seashore recognized Mahonri Moriancumer as their leader and considered themselves the people of Mahonri, then when did the people change and begin to recognize Jared as their leader and begin to call themselves the people of Jared? Was it when they built the barges, saw the shining stones, or crossed the sea? On the contrary, each of these events would have reinforced the people's understanding that Mahonri, not Jared, was their prophet and leader. So why and when did they take upon themselves the name "the people of Jared"?

One possibility is that when Orihah, the son of Jared, became the king of the people in the new world he may have directed the people to call themselves after his father (Orihah's reign is found in Ether 6:22–30, Ether 7:1). However, the record makes it clear that Orihah was a righteous king "all his days," and as such it would seem unlikely that he would rename his people without the consent or possibly even the direction of the prophet. During the initial part of Orihah's reign, the prophet would have been the brother of Jared, himself. After Orihah's reign, the people would have had no personal knowledge of either Jared or his brother and no reason to change the name of their nation. Thus, the most likely time that this change or renaming of the nation took place was when the brother of Jared was still alive. It most likely occurred at his own direction.

Throughout this book we postulate that it was by his own choice that the brother of Jared's name was not recorded. If the brother of Jared chose to be anonymous in the record and sought to redirect attention away from his name, he would not have wanted the nation named after him either. As such it would appear that when he chose to go into the record as the brother of Jared he also chose to rename the nation that he founded. The nation, along with himself, would honor the name of his brother, Jared. The people would be known as the people of Jared or in our day by the shorter term Jaredites.[1]

Why would this prophet and leader decide that he and the nation he founded would be known by the name of his brother? The answer to this may lie within the meaning of the name Jared itself. The name Jared is of Hebrew origin and is first found in the Old Testament in Genesis 5:15. The first man to be named Jared was the fifth generation below Adam and was the father of Enoch (see Genesis 5:15–20). In Hebrew, the name Jared is derived from the verb *yarad.* This is a commonly used verb that literally means to "go down" or "descend" as in "descend from the top of a mountain."[2] Thus, the name Jared literally means "he who goes down" or "one who descends." If the name Jared means "one who descends," then the term "the people of Jared" or "Jaredites" would be taken to mean "the people who descend" or "the descenders."

The Lord chose and directed the Jaredites to build barges and take the journey where they would descend below the depths of the sea. The Jaredite people, or "the people who descend," went below where any man had gone before. By fulfilling this foreordained calling, they received their inheritance in the promised land. It would appear that from the beginning the Lord had foreordained the Jaredite people to do this work. The Lord intended that the people would be known by what they accomplished rather than by who their leader was.

There may be another reason the brother of Jared may have desired that his people be known as the people of Jared. In his encounter with the Lord on the mount, the brother of Jared would have seen the condescension of the great Jehovah as He came down and walked on this earth. He would have viewed the suffering of the Savior in the Garden of Gethsemane as He bore the sins of the world. He would have seen His crucifixion and glorious resurrection on the third day. The brother of Jared would have seen that Jesus Christ was the One who "descended below all things" to bring about the salvation of mankind (D&C 88:6–7). Because the name Jared literally means "one who descends," the brother of Jared would have learned the name Jared is a type and a reminder of Jesus Christ Himself.

In that vision where he saw the condescension of Jesus Christ, the brother of Jared would also have seen each of his people through the eyes of Jesus Christ. He would have known their trials and understood their thoughts in a way that no other leader had ever experienced. His understanding and compassion for his people would have been multiplied. His greatest desire would be to honor them, bless them, and bring them to Christ.

The brother of Jared would have understood that his people had been chosen to descend on a journey that would symbolically and metaphorically remind them of the condescension and sacrifice of the Savior Himself. Because the name Jared was a type and a reminder of Christ and his sacrifice, it is fitting that he would choose to have the nation be known as the "people of Jared." It was his people who had built the barges that lacked light to see and the air needed for life. It was through these barges that the people learned that Jesus Christ is the "light, the life, and the truth of the world" (Ether 4:12). These barges had no way to steer or a direction to go, but the direction given unto them from Christ was to "Come unto me" (Ether 4:13–14). It would seem that the Lord wanted His people to take upon themselves a name that would remind them of who gave them light, life, and direction. This name would remind them that they were disciples of Jesus Christ.

NOTES

1. It is interesting to note that nowhere in the Book of Mormon are the people referred to as Jaredites. Moroni always refers to them as "the people of Jared." The term *Jaredites* or the use of the term *ite* may not have been a convention used by the people of Jared. Thus, the term *Jaredite* may be an element of Latter-day interpretation. It is clear, however, that the use of the term *Jaredite* is common and understood in the Church today as it is used throughout the chapter headings and index of the Book of Mormon, though not in the text itself.
2. Several web sources are available on origin of the name of Jared. One of the more interesting sources is Abarim Publications Biblical Name Vault (abarim-publications.com/Meaning/Jared.html#.XgyjD0dKiUk). Several baby naming websites also note the Hebrew source of the name Jared (nameberry.com/babyname/Jared).

Chapter 22

A CONSECRATED PEOPLE

In 1832, a group of Saints who were former followers of Sidney Rigdon gathered at the Morley farm near Kirtland, Ohio. These Saints desired to live the doctrines taught in the New Testament that described the Saints as having all things in common. In this experiment the people lived on the Morley farm and shared their resources. This society of Saints who shared all things worked for a period of time. However, at some point one of the brethren took a pocket watch that belonged to Levi Hancock and sold it without asking, causing contention among the group. In response to these events and the desire of the people to live a higher law, Joseph Smith inquired of the Lord and was given the doctrines of the law of consecration. Several attempts were made in Kirtland and Missouri to live the law of consecration but were unsuccessful. The people of the early Church were not yet prepared to live the higher laws of the gospel.

Many writers have pointed out the similarities between the experience that the brother of Jared had on the mountain and other recorded encounters between man and God. Like Moses on Mount Sinai and Peter on the Mount of Transfiguration, the brother of Jared certainly had a temple experience with the Savior on the mountain.[1] As such he may have left the mountaintop with more than shining stones and memories of his vision of eternity. He may have also left the mountain with the teachings of the higher laws of the gospel and the ordinances of the ancient temple similar to that contained in the law of Moses.

The people of Jared had been faithful. They repented of their sins. They followed the leadership of their prophet and worked diligently to construct the barges according to the Lord's instructions. The people were worthy of receiving the blessings of the ancient temples. Like the Latter-day Saints in Nauvoo, they would have needed and wanted these blessings prior to embarking on their dangerous journey.

Wherever a righteous people are gathered, the Lord and His prophet always desire to give them these blessings. We know that in ancient times, the Lord provided temple ordinances and blessings to Adam, Enoch, Moses, Nephi, and their people according to their worthiness.

In the case of the Jaredites, however, there was no record of a temple that was constructed. Perhaps the brother of Jared took his followers back up the mountain to provide them with these blessings. Perhaps, like Moses, he constructed a tabernacle-like structure using tents so the people could receive their ordinances while in the wilderness. However, another possibility remains. The barges themselves were designed by the Lord and filled with His light. Like a temple, the people had dedicated themselves to their construction in obedience to their God. It is possible that the barges themselves were dedicated to serve as a temple for the people.

What evidence do we have that the people of Jared received temple ordinances and obeyed the higher law? Like the early Saints of the latter-day Church we often consider the law of consecration to be a requirement that we donate or share our possessions. However, the law of consecration isn't about our belongings; it is about our hearts. The Lord requires that we consecrate our heart and our mind to building His kingdom. The early Saints of the Church failed to live the law of concentration because they tried to consecrate their material possessions before they learned to consecrate their hearts.

The Jaredites on the seashore had all the earthly possessions they needed. They could have ended their journey there and lived their own lives in a more than satisfactory condition. There is ample evidence to suggest that the people of Jared desired to stay on the seashore rather than cross the dangerous ocean. The Lord, however, knew their journey was not just about Jared, his brother, and the people participating in the journey. The Lord had a vision of building up a nation or a kingdom that would be greater than any other on the earth at that time (Ether 1:43). A kingdom that would flourish in righteousness for thousands of years with millions of people who would serve the God who created them. While the seashore was sufficient for a small group of travelers for a few generations, it would never suffice as a kingdom for God's people.

The Lord required the Jaredites to consecrate themselves for the purposes of building His kingdom. To do this, the people of Jared had to learn to love God, and their future posterity, more than they loved their own selves and their own comfortable situation. The people of Jared would have to consecrate their hearts and their minds, their time, and their labor to accomplishing God's work and building His kingdom. They had to sacrifice all they possessed in their old world in order to obtain the blessings of the new for their own posterity. Furthermore, we know that the Lord would never require such sacrifice from these people without promising the blessings that were predicated on obedience to this law. We know that the people of the Jaredites accepted and obeyed this covenant. Ether 6:4 states that in building the barges and crossing the ocean the people of Jared were "commending themselves unto the Lord their God." The people of Jared placed their own lives in the hands of the Lord so that they could attain the promised land and build the Lord's kingdom.

Of all the possessions we may have to consecrate to God's kingdom, the highest form of consecration is to consecrate ourselves to the Lord our God. The fact that the Jaredites consecrated themselves for the building of God's kingdom in the promised land is evidence that the people lived the higher laws of the gospel.

NOTE

1. Book of Mormon Central's "Why Did Moroni Use Temple Imagery While Telling the Brother of Jared Story?" discusses in depth the similarities between the brother of Jared's experience on the mount Shelem and the ancient temple ordinances (https://knowhy.bookofmormoncentral.org/knowhy/why-did-moroni-use-temple-imagery-while-telling-the-brother-of-jared-story).

Chapter 23

A PRAYER OF GRATITUDE IS A PRAYER OF FAITH

Throughout the story of the brother of Jared, we see how the Lord planned, prepared, and strengthened the faith of the brother of Jared so he could be redeemed and stand in His presence. It is interesting how the prayers of the brother of Jared reflected the changes and corresponding increase in his faith. This is particularly true during the journey across the ocean where the brother of Jared "did thank and praise the Lord all the day long" (Ether 6:9).

At the beginning of the story it is noted that the brother of Jared was a man who was "highly favored of the Lord." He was given the spiritual gift of leadership and prophecy. He was recognized by Jared and his people as one who could pray unto the Lord and receive answers and direction on behalf of the people. The brother of Jared had a relationship with the Lord that had grown from continual prayer. As the people prepared to leave Babel and as they journeyed in the wilderness, answers and direction were continually given to the brother of Jared. At the beginning, every question and every prayer were met with direction and answers as the people began their journey away from the city of Babel. The Lord noted that the prayers of the brother of Jared had been answered because of the "long time ye have cried unto me" (Ether 1:43).

As the people progressed in their journey with the Lord, they reached the seashore where they were instructed to build barges. Here, the brother of Jared encountered a new situation where the petitions of his prayers were not always answered in the way he expected. This would have been a new encounter for him, as up to this point the will of the Lord and the will of the people had always aligned. At the seashore, the people sought to build boats, but the Lord's plan was much greater—the Lord sought to build faith. In order to build faith, answers to the brother of Jared's prayers regarding the air, the light, and the steering would have to wait until the barges were complete. Hitherto, the Lord answered prayers because the brother of Jared had the faith to ask and sometimes ask for a "long time." Hereafter, the Lord would require both asking in faith and acting in faith before granting the desired direction.

When the brother of Jared and the people encountered this new situation where it appeared the Lord was no longer answering their prayers, their faith and their prayers faltered. They had come to expect the Lord to give them whatever they asked for. The story does not record what brought the brother of Jared back to Lord after four years. However, it is evident that even though the brother of Jared had given up on the Lord, the Lord had not given up on him. The Lord's faith in the brother of Jared far exceeded the faith that the brother of Jared had in himself or in the Lord.

Up to this time, the brother of Jared had brought the will of the people to the Lord. Now he needed to discern the will of the Lord and bring it to the people. This would have required a substantial change in his prayers. Instead of bending the will of the Lord to match the desires of the people, the brother of Jared needed to learn how to change and yield his own desires to match the will of the Lord. Furthermore, he would need to bend the hearts of the people to conform to the commandments given him from God.

After building the barges, the next recorded prayer of the brother of Jared showed that he and the people had indeed conformed to the will of the Lord and had "performed the work which thou (the Lord) hast commanded" (Ether 2:18–19). The Lord first responded to this prayer with a directive to provide air for the barges by making a hole in the top and in the bottom. Once the people had completed the directive of the Lord, the Lord responded to the next prayer by inviting the brother of Jared to suggest a solution to the lack of light within the barges (Ether 2:23). Having proven himself a worthy servant to the will of the Lord, the brother of Jared received an invitation to participate in the work of the Lord.

When the people of Jared first left Babel, the prayers of the brother of Jared had been the prayers of a beggar as he sought to turn away the wrath of the Lord and not confound their language. As they built the barges, his prayers had become as one of a servant seeking to submit his will and the will of the people to their master. As the brother of Jared approached the Lord with his stones, he initiated his prayer with the humility he had learned as a beggar and the submissiveness he had learned as a servant. He then presented his request to the Lord as a participant expressing full confidence and faith in the Lord to complete the work he had initiated to make stones shine in the darkness.

The humility, submissiveness, and confidence the brother of Jared had developed resulted in a faith that removed the veil from his eyes and revealed the finger of the Lord. Because of this knowledge, the Lord could not conceal Himself, and the brother of Jared was able to enter into His presence. In the Lord's presence he was no longer a beggar, servant, or participant. As a trusted friend the brother of Jared was invited to witness all of His creations and all of His children from the beginning to the end of time.

Following this experience, the Jaredites entered the barges and commended themselves unto the Lord their God. It is recorded that when "they were encompassed about by many waters they did cry unto the Lord, and he did bring them forth again upon the top of the waters. . . . And they did sing praises unto the Lord, yea the brother of Jared did sing praises unto the Lord and he did thank and praise the Lord all the day long; and when the night came, they did not cease to praise the Lord" (Ether 6:7–9).

The final evolution of the prayers of the brother of Jared and his people were prayers of continual gratitude. Even in the midst of great affliction being buried in the depths of the sea and suffering for air, the brother of Jared did not cease to thank and praise the Lord. Offering thankfulness and praise even in the midst of affliction is the highest form of faith. The prayer of continual gratitude even in affliction is not the prayer of a beggar, a servant, or a participant. A prayer of gratitude is offered when one realizes the Lord is a trusted friend and that no matter what occurs, the Lord will make all things for our good.

In the April 2014 general conference Elder Uchtdorf said:

> When we are grateful to God in our circumstances, we can experience gentle peace in the midst of tribulation. In grief, we can still lift up our hearts in praise. In pain, we can glory in Christ's Atonement. In the cold of bitter sorrow, we can experience the closeness and warmth of heaven's embrace. We sometimes think that being grateful is what we do after our problems are solved, but how terribly shortsighted that is. How much of life do we miss by waiting to see the rainbow before thanking God that there is rain?
>
> Being grateful in our circumstances is an act of faith in God. It requires that we trust God and hope for things we may not see but which are true. By being grateful, we follow the example of our beloved Savior, who said, "Not my will, but thine, be done."[1]

When Jesus approached the tomb of his friend Lazarus, He offered a prayer of thanks to His Father (John 11: 41–42). It would seem that this would be an unusual time to offer thanks as his friend had died and no miracle had yet occurred. But Jesus set the example of offering gratitude to our Father in Heaven in the midst of our deepest afflictions. The Savior's expression of gratitude was offered regardless of the outcome of the fate of his friend. As such, the offering of gratitude in any situation is the ultimate prayer of faith and trust that the Father will turn all things for our good. Perhaps an honest prayer of gratitude in our afflictions is even more influential in swaying the will of the Lord to our desired outcome than a prayer of begging or desperation. A prayer of gratitude as demonstrated by the Savior may even be necessary in order to obtain the most difficult of miracles or receive the greatest of blessings.

When we find ourselves in desperate need of the Lord's help, we can alter our prayers to become a prayer of gratitude and faith by thinking back on a time when the Lord had previously blessed us, our friends, or our family when in similar desperate situations. We can then thank the Lord for His past mercies and express faith that He will continue to go with us in our current struggles. We can thank Him for our knowledge that He will make all things for our good, including our current desperate situation. We can commit to the Lord that we will accept His will and continue to move forward trusting in Him, despite our difficulty. In this way, we can express our needs to the Lord and yet alter our prayers from one of desperation and demands to a prayer of thankfulness and faith. We can consciously change our prayers from that of a beggar or a servant to the prayer of a trusting friend.

Jesus Christ loves each of us and considers us to be His friends. In Doctrine and Covenants 84:77 He even commands us to become his friends: "And again I say unto you, my friends, for from henceforth I shall call you friends, it is expedient that I give unto you this commandment, that ye become even as my friends in days when I was with them, traveling to preach the gospel in my power."

Even though Jesus considers us His friends, we must choose to bring Him into our lives and accept His offer to be our friend. We must allow ourselves to trust Him enough to develop that friendship with Him. Our expressions of gratitude in our personal prayers are one of the best indicators of the true state of our relationship with our Savior.

Throughout the story of the brother of Jared, the prayers of the brother of Jared progressed from that of a beggar, to a servant, to a participant, and ultimately to that of a trusted friend of the Lord Jesus Christ. The brother of Jared's continual prayer of gratitude and thanks to his Savior and friend brought about the greatest miracle and delivered the Jaredites from the depths of the sea to the shores of the promised land.

NOTE

1. Dieter F. Uchtdorf, "Grateful in Any Circumstances," *Ensign*, May 2013.

Chapter 24

THE LORD WOULD NOT SUFFER

The Jaredites accomplished their foreordained destiny and crossed the sea to obtain their promised land. Throughout this book we note that the promised land is symbolic of the celestial kingdom. If the promised land is the celestial kingdom of the story of Jared, then what lands represent the telestial and terrestrial kingdoms? Given its worldly ways, we can safely assume that the city of Babel would be representative of the telestial kingdom. If the promised land is celestial and Babel is telestial, then the land that represents the terrestrial kingdom would be the seashore in the wilderness.

When Jared first left Babel, he was inspired to seek a land that was choice above all other lands. Such was his determination to obtain his land of promise. Jared essentially made a covenant that he and his people would be "faithful unto the Lord, that we may receive it for (their) inheritance" (Ether 1:38). The Lord accepted the covenant of Jared and fulfilled his part of the promise as He directed the Jaredites on their journey from Babel to the seashore and from the seashore to the promised land.

The Jaredites arrived at the seashore but soon found that the journey from the seashore to the promised land was the most difficult of all journeys. At the seashore, the Jaredites realized that the ocean waves were deep, the submersible barges were dark, and their covenant of the promised land seemed distant. The oppression of the telestial Babel was behind them, and the seashore of the terrestrial world was appealing. They had sandy beaches, beautiful sunsets, and plenty of fish. The terrestrial seashore appealed to the Jaredites as an acceptable place to end their journey. Perhaps they pleaded with the Lord to allow them to stay on their comfortable seashore and not build the barges. Despite the complacency of the Jaredites, the Lord still remembered the promise of His people: "The Lord would not suffer that they should stop beyond the sea in the wilderness, but he would that they should come forth even unto the land of promise, which was choice above all other lands" (Ether 2:7).

In the eyes of the Lord there is no second best. There is no kingdom worth inhabiting if it is not His celestial kingdom. As such, allowing the Jaredites to abandon their journey on the terrestrial seashore was not acceptable to the Lord. In the eyes of the Lord, a covenant was made, and He would not suffer His people to break their covenant and abandon the promised land. It is not recorded what persuasions the Lord made or trials He sent to convince the Jaredites to leave the seashore and restart their journey to the promised land. However, the Lord did everything He could, within the confines of man's agency, to convince the Jaredites to move forward and cross the ocean. Every persuasion, hardship, challenge, and trial was given with one purpose—to convince his people to come to Him in the covenanted celestial "promised land."

Before coming to earth, each of us saw the glory of the Father and desired to be like Him, no matter what difficulties we had to endure. Like Jared, each of us promised that we would be faithful to the Lord so that we could become like Him and attain His kingdom. Our Father's proposal of the plan of salvation and the offering of His Son showed that He approved of our promise, and He provided the plan. Thus, our acceptance of our Father's plan of salvation was, in essence, our first covenant. Elder Christofferson called this our "premortal commitment" and said that "your physical birth is testament to the fact that you already committed."[1] Our Father in Heaven and His Son, Jesus Christ, have fulfilled their part of this covenant. They expect us to keep ours.

After we came to this earth and passed through the veil, the memory of our Father was diminished. On this earth we experience the depravity of the telestial world, and most of us want to live above it. Our determination to live the basic principles of Christianity qualifies our soul for the terrestrial realm. It is easy to feel that because we are living a better existence than the telestial, our journey is sufficient. The terrestrial realm seems inviting and satisfies our earthly needs. However, the promised land of the celestial feels distant and difficult. To get there we know that, like the Jaredites, we would have to commend our whole souls unto the Lord.

The Lord has compared the glory of the kingdoms to the glory of the sun, moon, and stars. In a forensic investigation we may use a light meter to measure the light available in various conditions. The light measured is described in terms of foot-candles defined as the light given by one candle that is one foot away from the observer. Using this standard, the light of the brightest starlight is measured at 0.0001 foot candles, and the light from a full moon is measured at 0.01 foot candles, or 100 times brighter than the stars. Would we be content living in the light of the moon simply because it is 100 times better than the light of the stars? Would we be content in a terrestrial existence simply because it is better than the telestial world we know?

The light from the sun, however, is measured at 10,000 foot candles or one million times as bright as the brightest moonlight. In comparison to the sun, the light from the moon and the light from the stars are almost equal and nearly inconsequential. Our Father in Heaven knows the glory of the celestial kingdom even though we have forgotten. He desires nothing less for us. When we lived with Him and knew Him, we covenanted we would achieve nothing less than His glory no matter what trials were required in this earthly classroom.

Many of us, like the Jaredites, are content with a terrestrial existence. We are comfortable living on a seashore that is a mere 100 times better than the telestial Babel. We may have beautiful beaches, orange sunsets, and trees with fruit, but we know in our hearts that the seashore is not our eternal destiny. As such, it

Common Light Levels Outdoor

Common light levels outdoor at day and night can be found in the table below.

Condition	Illumination (ftcd)	Illumination (lux)
Sunlight	10,000	107,527
Full Daylight	1,000	10,752
Overcast Day	100	1,075
Very Dark Day	10	107
Twilight	1	10.8
Deep Twilight	.1	1.08
Full Moon	.01	.108
Quarter Moon	.001	.0108
Starlight	.0001	.0011
Overcast Night	.00001	.0001

Outdoor light levels measured in English measurements of foot-candles (ftcd) and the metric measurement of lux (courtesy of engineeringtoolbox.com).

seems we are still "dwelling in tents" on the proverbial terrestrial seashore uncommitted to the next journey. However, the Lord will do everything He can within the confines of our agency to convince us to move forward. Every persuasion, hardship, challenge, and trial is given with the intent to convince us to keep our covenant and come to Him in His celestial kingdom. Joseph Smith said: "A religion that does not require the sacrifice of all things never has power sufficient to produce the faith necessary unto life and salvation . . . through this sacrifice, and this only, God has ordained that men should enjoy eternal life."[2]

Our spiritual journey to the celestial promised land is not easy. However, in our hearts we know that an eternity without our Father in Heaven and without our families would never bring true light and happiness. Despite our trials and unanswered questions, we, like the Jaredites, must commit to building our barges. Some of our barges have physical difficulties that make us feel as if we are lacking for air. Others have spiritual challenges that seem to be void of light. At times we may feel that we have been asked to construct the vessel of our own demise. However, faith is built by continuing the construction. We must build whatever barge the Lord, in his wisdom, has placed before us despite the obvious defects. By driving the next nail and cutting the next board, we build our faith like the brother of Jared. We build the faith necessary for us to commit our souls and complete our journey. It is through these small actions of faith that the Lord has a plan to perfect our souls and bring us back to Him in His celestial kingdom.

Most earthly religions consider our journey on earth to be a test to determine if we can qualify for heaven. Through our experiences we learn that life is the perfect classroom where we can learn, experience, and grow to prepare ourselves for the promised land. However, the construction of our barges and our journey here on earth is more than a test or a classroom—it is the fulfilling of our covenant. We promised the Father that we would return to Him, no matter what hardships we face in this classroom of life. Our Father also covenanted with us that He would do all in His power to help us return, even offering the sacrifice of His beloved Son to fulfill his perfect plan. Like the Jaredites, the Lord will not suffer that we should break our covenant and stop short of His promised land.

NOTES

1. Elder Christofferson discussed our "premortal commitment" in a talk given on January 12, 2020, at Utah Valley University. (See churchofjesuschrist.org/church/news/choose-committing-to-christ-over-fear-of-missing-out-elder-christofferson-tells-young-adults?lang=eng.)
2. Joseph Smith *Lectures on Faith* (Salt Lake City: Deseret Book, 1985) 6:7.

Chapter 25

THE BROTHER OF JARED, A BROTHER OF JESUS

In The Church of Jesus Christ of Latter-day Saints, we attach great meaning to names. We give our child a name and a blessing at birth. We research the names of our ancestors. We present both our names and the names of our ancestors before the Lord as we perform ordinances in His temples. We take upon us the name of Christ, and all that we do is done in His name. We are taught not to glorify our own name but to give glory to the name of the Lord.

The wicked people of Babel, inspired by Satan, sought to exalt their own name by building a tower to enter God's presence. It is apparent the Lord intended that the Jaredite record provide a spiritual contrast to the wicked people of Babel. As the prideful purpose of the people of Babel was to exalt their own name, the Lord chose a humble man who was willing to sacrifice his own name for the glory of God.

Many of the ancient prophets who entered into the presence of God were given new names by the Lord following their encounter with Deity. Abram was given the name Abraham, or "father of many," after his encounter with the Lord. Jacob was given the name Israel. Simon was given the name Peter, or "the rock," and continues to be known by that name.

Certainly the brother of Jared's experience in the presence of Jesus Christ had a similar impact on him. In that encounter, he learned of the condescension, sacrifice, and resurrection of the Savior. He saw the descension of his people in the barges as a type of the Savior's sacrifice. As the name Jared means "one who descends," it is a fitting description of both his people and his Savior. Being known by the name "the brother of Jared" would reflect both his relationship with his earthly brother and his love for his heavenly one. Perhaps, like other prophets, the direction and inspiration to do so came from the Lord Himself.

The Lord directed the brother of Jared to write this vision in a confounded language and hide it from the world. His name would be sealed with the record he wrote. Yet, the time will come when the vision of the brother of Jared will be revealed to all who have faith in the Lord Jesus Christ. As the light from the stones filled the Jaredite barges of old, the light from this vision will fill the whole earth with the knowledge of God. When that time comes, the world will know whose vision it was.

Regardless of the reason his name was hidden, this story is more about man's relationship with Deity than about a specific individual. Perhaps it is fitting that the brother of Jared is known by a relationship rather than by a specific name.

In the Church of Jesus Christ, we often talk about our testimony as something we know. We may say we have a testimony if we "know the church is true" or if we "know that Jesus is the Christ." The reality is that knowledge alone will not bring us back into the presence of God, for the "devils also believe and tremble" (James 2:19). More important than our testimony or knowledge of truth is our relationship with Jesus Christ. Eternal life is not knowing *of* Christ but personally *knowing Him* (John 17:3). It is incumbent upon each of us to seek out and develop that relationship through prayer, faith, and action.

The story of the brother of Jared is really the story of each of us as we seek to develop our own personal relationship with our brother Jesus Christ. As such it may be said that each of us is, in fact, a brother of one who descends. All of us who are disciples of Christ, who descended below all things, could metaphorically be considered Jaredites.

The story of the brother of Jared gives us a pattern for developing our own relationship with the Savior. Specifically, it gives us an example of developing faith and increasing the spirituality of our prayers. Each of us in our own way has been commanded to "go to work and build." Whether we build barges, buildings, educations, careers, families, relationships, endurance, or patience, our purpose is to build faith in our brother Jesus Christ. At some point each of us will find we cannot possibly understand the purpose of our repetitive, aimless actions unless we rely on the Lord. Only He can provide answers and touch our stony heart when we have completed the work He has asked us to do.

In our assigned work we will encounter challenges, trials, defects, and difficulties that are not unlike the problems encountered by the people of Jared. The things that we perceive as flaws in the world or weaknesses in our own souls are actually part of the great eternal plan to bring us back into the Lord's presence. The three defects in the barges are representative of the needs we encounter in life. In our assigned work, we must go to the Lord at times to request assistance with our physical needs (air), spiritual needs (light), and direction in our lives (steering). The answers that the Lord gives us as we seek for guidance will likely be similar to the answers given to the brother of Jared. As we move forward in faith, He will give us direction, seek our participation, or reveal the answers when we have completed the work we were assigned to do. After we have done all we can do, then His grace is sufficient to take care of the rest.

Thus, it may be that the reason the name of the brother of Jared is not given is that he and the Lord wanted this story to be about us. When the brother of Jared saw the inhabitants of the earth, he saw each of us. He knew who we were. He knew the love Jesus Christ has for each of us. This story teaches us about our relationship with Deity and our potential to know God and stand in His presence. Through this we can develop our relationship with Jesus Christ as our brother and our Savior and know He has descended below all things to bring His salvation to us.

Chapter 26

AN ANCIENT STORY FOR OUR DAY

There are many unanswered questions about The Church of Jesus Christ of Latter-day Saints. Some faithful Saints struggle with the Church's position on different topics that seem to conflict with the world's understanding. Some may have unexplainable trials with mental health, physical illnesses, or personal loss. In many of these issues the prophets acknowledge the Lord has not provided answers or explanations. Without these answers, some have become complacent or ceased their activity in the Church with the expectation that a perfect God would certainly know how to establish a perfect church.

In this story, we learn there was a period of time when the brother of Jared also may have struggled in his assignments and relationship with the Lord. While we do not know all the details regarding his difficulty, it is possible the brother of Jared had not prayed for a number of years. In the membership of the Church today, there are many who have questions, have ceased activity, and have also struggled in their relationship with the Lord. These may be the people the story of the brother of Jared would help the most.

The brother of Jared likely became frustrated with the Lord when he discovered the defects in the plan for the barges. Like many of the people in our day, the brother of Jared expected that a perfect God would provide perfect plans for perfect barges. When he discovered the plans were not perfect, he demanded an explanation from the Lord, but no answers came.

All the initial actions of the brother of Jared in refusing to build defective barges were logical within his telestial understanding, and yet the Lord had a celestial plan. The Lord was not interested in building barges. The Lord was building perfect faith.

Likewise, in our day many struggle or have become inactive in the Church because they expect a perfect God would provide perfect plans for a perfect church. However, the Lord's plan is not about building a church. The Lord's plan is once again about building faith.

Like the barges of old, the church we are building may appear to have imperfect answers to difficult questions. To some, participating in a church without complete answers may feel like building a vessel with no air to breathe, nor light to see. In these times we must trust the Lord and our prophet and continue in the construction. Perhaps, like the Jaredites, these unanswered questions exist within the Church to give us an opportunity to build faith that can be obtained no other way. Perhaps these questions exist to give the Lord an opportunity to show us the many miracles He intends for us to receive.

If the brother of Jared is our example, there may be people with great spiritual and leadership potential who are experiencing a trial of faith or are inactive because of concerns or questions they may have. Their frustration with the Church may be perfectly logical in our telestial realm, yet we know the Lord has a celestial plan. Like the brother of Jared, the Lord has the capacity to take the experiences and lessons learned during years of questions or inactivity and turn these weaknesses into strengths to increase our faith and bring about our salvation.

Likewise, as faithful members of the Church, we may yet experience afflictions, illness, or trials of faith that may lead us to question the intent of the Lord. In these times, the example of the brother of

Jared can give us strength as we learn to trust the Lord and build our own faith. The pattern of prayer offered by the brother of Jared can help us find gratitude in the midst of our afflictions.

In his vision of mankind, the brother of Jared saw all the people who would inhabit the earth. He must have had great compassion for these people who were experiencing trials of faith, who questioned the Lord's plan, or who had become inactive in their relationship with the Lord. The brother of Jared had deep empathy for these people as he also struggled in his faith and allowed himself to become separated from the Lord during his years on the seashore. Just as the Lord did not forget or give up on the brother of Jared, it is certain that the Lord has not forgotten or given up on us.

Chapter 27

GO TO WORK AND BUILD—A KINGDOM

In the 1830s it was revealed to the Prophet Joseph Smith that Zion, the New Jerusalem, was to be built in Independence, Missouri. The people of the Church moved to Independence in great numbers as they sought to build Zion, their modern-day promised land. They were met with contention that resulted in members being expelled from Missouri and the United States. Since that time, members of The Church of Jesus Christ of Latter-Day Saints have metaphorically wandered in the wilderness as the Lord prepares His people for the promised land.

Although we know that one day the New Jerusalem will be built in Missouri, the Lord has revealed that the true Zion is more than a place. It is a people; a people who are living in a state of love, unity, and purity throughout the world. We know that preparing His people is the work of the Lord. As such our prophet has again received a commandment to "go to work and build" a kingdom—the kingdom of God. This kingdom will encompass the whole earth with a people who are prepared to receive the return of their King—the Lord and Savior Jesus Christ.

The instructions the Lord has given for His kingdom are different from any previous earthly kingdom or government. Many people inside and outside the Church have looked at the instructions for building His kingdom and declared them to be unusual or incomplete. The world has declared the plans presented by the prophets to have irredeemable flaws.

Like the barges in the story of the brother of Jared, the modern-day instructions the Lord has given for building His church may be missing components or information that in our limited telestial knowledge we may view to be defects. The answers to some questions regarding the Church may even be withheld according to the wisdom of the Lord. However, the Lord's plan isn't about building a church. His purpose is to save His people by building their faith. The plan of the Lord to prepare His people is perfect. We must trust the Lord and continue to construct His kingdom. The church we build will one day be touched by the Master and all flaws and shortcomings will be dispersed by the glorious light of His presence. Through His miracles, the church built by our faith and blessed by His hand will become a vessel of our salvation.

Just as the people of Jared increased their faith by building barges they perceived to be flawed, we too must exercise faith and "go to work and build" His kingdom according to His plan. Many of us have faltered in our prayers, been sidelined on the seashore, or have hesitated to commend our souls to His direction. Yet, like the Jaredites of old, each of us has a work to do. Each of us has our own barges of faith to build. We have been chosen and foreordained to build the kingdom of God on earth and to prepare the people of the earth for the Second Coming of Jesus Christ. By commending our souls to Him and continuing in His work, we are building our faith like the brother of Jared. In Ether 4:7–19 we read:

> And in that day that they shall exercise faith in me, saith the Lord, even as the brother of Jared did, that they may become sanctified in me, then will I manifest unto them the things which the brother of Jared saw, even to the unfolding unto them all my revelations saith Jesus Christ, the Son of God, the Father of the heavens and of the earth, and all things that in them are. . . .

> For behold, I am the Father, I am the light, and the life and the truth of the world.
>
> Come unto me, O ye Gentiles and I will show unto you the greater things, the knowledge which is hid up because of unbelief
>
> Come unto me, O ye house of Israel, and it shall be made manifest unto you how great things the Father hath laid up for you, from the foundation of the world; and it hath not come unto you because of unbelief.
>
> Behold, when ye shall rend that veil of unbelief which doth cause you to remain in your awful state of wickedness, and hardness of heart, and blindness of mind, then shall the great and marvelous things which have been hid up from the foundation of the world from you—yea, when ye shall call upon the Father in my name, with a broken heart and a contrite spirit, then shall ye know that the Father hath remembered the covenant which he made unto your fathers, O house of Israel. . .
>
> Therefore repent all ye ends of the earth, and come unto me and believe in my gospel, and be baptized in my name. . .
>
> And blessed is he that is found faithful unto my name at the last day, for he shall be lifted up to dwell in the kingdom prepared for him from the foundation of the world. And behold it is I that has spoken it. Amen.

The miracles and visions the brother of Jared experienced are unparalleled in the scriptures. However, we know the record of these events were written to prepare us for these latter days. Every prophet through the ages has testified of and rejoiced in our day. The blessings and miracles to come will be the most marvelous to occur since the time Christ walked on the earth. The brother of Jared built his faith so he could find heaven and enter the Lord's presence. As members of The Church of Jesus Christ of Latter-day Saints, we must build our faith so we can dwell in His presence when Christ returns to claim His heavenly kingdom.

Appendix A

A SUMMARY OF THIS BOOK

1. We need to know how to build our faith like the brother of Jared so that we can dwell in the presence of God.
2. There is only one name by which man can enter into the presence of God—the name of the Lord Jesus Christ.
3. We must be willing to sacrifice our own name and our own will to take upon us the name of Christ
4. The brother of Jared and the Jaredite nation provide a contrast to Satan's wicked kingdom of Babel.
5. The Jaredite people were intelligent and creative people who could do anything they imagined. They were faithful in following the Lord's directions through the wilderness to the seashore.
6. The Jaredites knew the seashore was not the promised land and knew they needed to cross the ocean from the day they arrived at the seashore.
7. The Seashore Theory states:

    a. The Lord gave instruction and a plan to build the barges and the people of Jared commenced building the barges when they first arrived at the seashore.

b. During the four-year period on the seashore, the brother of Jared faltered in his prayers. The people of Jared likewise faltered in their assignment to build the barges and eventually abandoned the effort.

c. The brother of Jared and the Jaredites were highly intelligent people who quickly recognized the deficiencies in the barges prior to the first one being completed.

d. The brother of Jared requested that the Lord provide the answers to the apparent defects in the barges early in the process, but the Lord chose not to answer as a trial of the Jaredites faith.

e. The apparent defects in the Lord's design of the barges and the lack of additional direction from the Lord contributed to the people abandoning the construction of the barges and the brother of Jared's faltering in his prayers.

f. The Jaredites may have experienced sickness, loss, or other trials of their faith during the four years on the seashore which also contributed to their separation from the Lord.

8. The Lord Jesus Christ knows how to build barges, and as such the defects in the plans for the barges were specific and intentional.

9. The experiences and shortcomings, and subsequent repentance that the brother of Jared, and the Jaredite people encountered during their four years on the seashore, were part of the plan and were instrumental in developing the character and faith of the brother of Jared and his people as the Lord prepared them for the Promised Land.

10. The Lord was most concerned with the brother of Jared's failure to pray and failure to repent. Ceasing to pray and refusing to repent is a form of denying the Holy Ghost and can lead to ripening in iniquity and loss of

one's inheritance in the kingdom of God if we do not repent.

11. The Lord's plan was not to build perfect boats but to build perfect faith in His people.

12. The Lord's plan for the Jaredite people was for them to recognize early on that the barges were non-functional and useless, but for the people to build the barges, and their faith, by putting their trust in the Lord and building the barges anyway.

13. It was the plan of the Lord from the beginning that through the construction of these useless barges, the brother of Jared was able to increase his faith and grow from an un-praying and inactive man into a prophet who was able to stand in the presence of the Lord.

14. Physical action is necessary to "exercise our faith." The plan for our salvation includes increasing our faith by taking physical action. The brother of Jared and the Jaredites exercised their faith by taking action and building the barges according to the commandments of the Lord, despite knowing their defects.

15. The Lord used the intentional defects in the barges to turn weaknesses into strengths. Each of the defects in the barges were designed by the Lord to enhance the faith of the people and give them evidence of the hand of the Lord in order to build the faith of the people and prepare them for the journey to the promised land.

16. The touch of Jesus Christ can fix any defect that exists in the work of our hands, or in the weaknesses of our hearts.

17. The Lord had a specific plan for the redemption and salvation of the brother of Jared and his people. He likewise has a specific plan for each of us.

18. If the Lord would have answered the initial prayers of the brother of Jared regarding the air, the light and the steering, it would have negated the Lord's overall plan to redeem the people of Jared and bring the brother of Jared back into His presence.

19. The Lord's foreordained plan for the brother of Jared was greater than any accomplishment or reward he could possibly imagine. Likewise, the Lord's foreordained plan and reward for us is greater than anything we can imagine.

20. Just as Jesus Christ knew the brother of Jared, He knows us personally and has suffered for each one of us. Having faith in Him is the most precious gift that we can give to Him in return.

21. The Lord asked the people of Jared to be willing to sacrifice everything to follow the prophet and attain the promised land. They commended their souls to the Lord their God. No sacrifice is too great in our pursuit of the kingdom of heaven.

22. No one is forgotten or left behind in the plan of the Lord. The salvation of the lowliest Jaredite was just as important to the Lord as was the salvation of the brother of Jared.

23. The brother of Jared decided that both he and the nations would be known by the name of his brother. As the name Jared is a type and reminder of Christ, being known as the people of Jared would remind them that they were disciples of Christ.

24. The Jaredite people had to give everything they had in the old world in order to obtain the new. More specifically, they consecrated themselves to building the kingdom of God in the new world.

25. The purpose of prayer is to develop a relationship with the Lord. The Lord desires a relationship with us and desires that through prayer we come to know and trust Him as a friend, for this is eternal life.

26. In the premortal life we promised or covenanted with our Father that we would follow Christ and return unto Him. Having faith in our promise, our Father prepared the plans of salvation and sent his Son to atone for our sins. Our Father in Heaven and Jesus Christ have kept their end of the covenant. They expect us to keep ours. They will not suffer that we break our promise and come short of the celestial kingdom.

27. Jesus Christ descended below all things in our behalf, and thus the name Jared, or "one who descends," is a symbol or type of Jesus Christ. As a followers of Jesus Christ we are, in a sense, "Jaredites."

28. The story of the brother of Jared applies to us today as there are many questions in the Church that require us to have faith and move forward. By doing so we will receive great miracles that the Lord has planned for us.

29. Like the Jaredites of old we have been chosen and fore-ordained to live in this time and "go to work and build" the kingdom of God on earth in preparation for the Second Coming of Jesus Christ.

Appendix B

COMPARING THE PEOPLE OF BABEL TO THE JAREDITES

Babel	Jaredites
The people of Babel sought to enter heaven.	The Jaredites entered into the promised land.
The leaders of Babel sought to enter God's presence.	The brother of Jared saw God and entered His presence.
The people of Babel sought to build a tower that would extend higher into the heavens than any building ever built.	The Jaredites built barges that would descend deeper into the sea than any vessel ever built.
The leaders of Babel sought to make their name famous.	The brother of Jared's name was not made known in the record.
The capacity of the people of Babel was such that they could do anything they imagined.	God's plan for His people was more incredible than the Jaredites' greatest imagination.
With one decree from God, the construction of the Tower of Babel was thwarted and the people of Babel were scattered.	By one touch from God's finger the barges were redeemed from their lack of light and the Jaredites were united.

The language of the people of Babel was confounded to stop their attempt to discover God and His secrets.	The brother of Jared discovered all the secrets of God but recorded it in a confounded language.
The failures of Babel to build their tower, attain heaven, and discover God are known throughout the world.	The vision of the brother of Jared was written in the sealed portion of the golden plates and remains unknown to the world.
Never had there been greater pride than was found in the leaders of Babel.	Never had there been greater humility and faith than was found in the brother of Jared.
The leaders of Babel thought that their ability to discover God was greater than God's ability to conceal Himself.	The brother of Jared's faith was so great that God could not keep Him from beholding within the veil.
The Tower of Babel was designed by men to reach heaven but was void of spiritual light.	The barges were designed by God for man to reach the promised land. They were filled with light that was given by His touch.
The city of Babel thought itself to be the "gate of God."	Baptism is the true gate to the heavenly path. The Jaredites' barges were immersed in the sea on their journey to the promised land symbolic of baptism.
Satan put these things into their heart.	God led and directed His people continually.
The people of Babel were scattered and the city left desolate due to the hand of Satan.	The Jaredites were redeemed and saved in the promised land by the hand of Jesus Christ.